Real Havana:

Explore Cuba Like A Local And Save Money

With Trinidad Bonus Section

Written and researched by

Mario Rizzi

About Full Compass Guides

Full Compass Guides are aimed at travelers who want to understand local customs and culture so that they can experience destinations like a local. Unlike regular *tourist guides*, Full Compass guides are **not** a list of hundreds of attractions popular with tourists, and boring restaurant and hotel reviews that are obsolete the moment they are published. With our guides, you get succinct, useful information about the culture, people and geography of your destination so you have the tools and the confidence to explore on your own, experience everything that your destination has to offer, and save money.

Our guides are written by experienced travelers who have intimate knowledge of both the location and the culture of the destination. They give you the exact information you need in order to make the most of your travel time.

<u>With a Full Compass guide, you will be a knowledgeable explorer, rather than just another flash-happy tourist.</u>

About the Author

This guide was written by Mario Rizzi, an award winning Canadian author. He first visited Cuba in 2007 and fell in love with the island. Since then he has returned dozens of times and considers Havana to be his second home.

He has explored every corner of the island, from the major cities to rural communities, and has become intimately acquainted with Cuban culture and lifestyle. Some of his closest friends are Cuban, and they have played an important role in his understanding of the island and the development of his Cuban guide series.

Mario is an avid traveler and his most important goal is to familiarize himself with the culture of a country so that he can explore it like a local would, rather than as a tourist. It often takes a great deal of time and effort to develop this understanding and as such, thriftiness is an important consideration.

In this guide, Mario boils down the complicated nuances of Cuban culture and daily life. The goal is to help the reader better understand Cuba and to explore the island, and particularly the city of Havana, like a local.

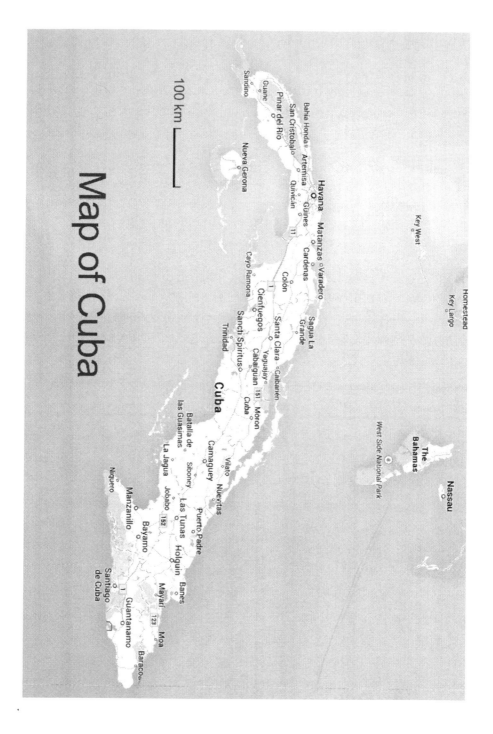

Map of Cuba

Table Of Contents

6

Introduction

One of the most common complaints I hear from tourists who have visited Cuba is that despite the country being poor, the trip is very expensive. Most of the foreigners who remark this are people who go to Cuba intending to experience lavish parties and to live at the highest standards, with all the amenities and creature comforts they enjoy in their home country. Naturally, these luxuries do not come cheap. If you throw money around, locals will gladly accept it. That goes for any country in the world.

But one of the best things about Cuba is that you absolutely do not have to spend a lot of money in order to have a lot of fun. Local Cubans earn a monthly wage equivalent to about $30 USD, yet they find ways to party with friends, explore the island and live a happy life. As a foreigner you will not be able to perfectly replicate all facets of Cuban life, in terms of cheap living, but you can easily experience most of it.

This book will explain in detail some of the best ways to explore Cuba and the city of Havana, most of which are free or inexpensive. You will rediscover simple joys which are often overlooked in our fast paced, modern lives. You will see how and where the average Cuban citizen finds pleasure and happiness.

But this guide does much more than simply give you tips. It will also develop your understanding of the Cuban culture and way of life, allowing you to gain insight into the Cuban identity and the local mindset. This will enable you to explore the culture on a level that most foreigners never consider, and help you experience the authentic Cuba from a local perspective. Furthermore, this infrastructure of knowledge will open many doors for you to independently discover your own money saving options.

Exploring Havana and Cuba cheaply can definitely be done and you don't have to look like a Cuban or speak fluent Spanish to accomplish it. With a reasonable degree of sensibility and cultural awareness, you can amplify your spending power on the island many times over. In a nutshell, that is what this book enables you to do. With Cuba experiencing such rapid and dramatic change, the time to visit and start your exploration is now, before it is too late.

Tips on Using This Guide

In order to view hundreds of <u>photos</u> and <u>videos</u> of Cuba, as well as listings and pictures of all the *Casas Particulares* which are reviewed at the end of this guide, simply go to the website:

<u>www.BestCubaGuide.com</u>

As a purchaser of this book, you now have a free, lifetime membership to this fantastic resource. It's packed with information on Havana and Cuba.

Any questions you may have can be posted in the forum, and will be answered quickly.

All the rental properties mentioned in this guide can be booked directly on the website, and you can also find dozens of great taxi deals and discounts. **Check it out!**

Background Information On Cuban Society

In order to integrate yourself at least a bit into Cuban society, you must know something about the history of the country and the daily Cuban way of life. This section will give you a superficial understanding of the Cuban social environment which you can then develop further as you read this guide. This knowledge will be immensely useful if your goal is to experience the authentic Cuba, not just the facade that is shown to regular tourists and foreigners.

Quick History Lesson

Cuba was one of the first islands explored by Christopher Columbus on his initial voyage to North America. At that time, the island was inhabited by Native American Indians called the *Taíno*. Columbus claimed the island for the Kingdom of Spain and colonization ensued. Fighting and outbreaks of disease eventually wiped out most of the native population, which had, by some estimates, exceeded 350 000 people.

The original capital of the country was located in Santiago de Cuba, which is currently Cuba's second largest city, located on the South-East coast of the island. Later, the capital city was changed to Havana. Throughout the 18th and 19th century, the country's population boomed as black slaves were brought in to work the lucrative sugar cane and tobacco fields. Eventually, there were rebellions and the citizens of Cuba revolted against the Spanish authority. Although their initial efforts to gain independence were unsuccessful, slavery was abolished by the 1880's.

The effort to gain independence from Spain was reinvigorated by the Cuban writer, José Marti, who started the Cuban Revolutionary Party in 1892. Fighting between Cubans and the Spanish accelerated in early 1895. José Marti was killed shortly after, in battle, solidifying his position as a freedom fighter and hero. The conflicts lasted for over a decade, resulting in the deaths of up to 400 000

Cuban civilians. Eventually, the United States joined the fight in support of Cuba, leading to the Spanish-American War.

In 1902, Cuba achieved independence from Spain. However, under the constitution, the United States retained strong governing authority over the island. Over the next three decades, tensions grew within Cuba as a series of US influenced, puppet governments took power and social reform stagnated. A political coup in 1933 resulted in Fulgencio Batista becoming president. Initially Batista was praised, as his government implemented a series of positive social reforms. Unfortunately, however, his desire for power soon put him at odds with the populace. Through another series of puppet governments, Batista retained de-facto control of Cuba well after his initial term as president expired, while also retaining close relations with the United States government. Batista ran for office again in 1952, and lost. A military coup followed and Batista became dictator of the country. The United States legitimized his power grab by almost immediately recognizing his regime.

At the time, Cuba was one of the most prosperous nations in Latin America, although income inequality was extremely high. During Batista's reign as dictator, his focus shifted away from social reform to catering predominantly to Cuba's upper class, and building his own personal fortune. Cuba went from a constitutional democracy to a dictatorial police state. Batista fostered a strong relationship with American crime syndicates and opened up the country to rampant corruption, large scale gambling, prostitution, drug smuggling and money laundering. Further antagonizing the average working class citizens was the fact that the vast majority of Cuban industry was owned and controlled by large American business interests.

From the social outrage, the seeds of a revolution were born. From 1953 to 1959, led by a charismatic lawyer named Fidel Castro, a rag tag team of fighters engaged in guerrilla warfare against the Batista regime. Despite a short incarceration, Fidel Castro, along with his brother Raul and the popular Che Guevara, with the help of a small, ill-equipped army, eventually were victorious, and Batista relinquished power and fled Cuba in 1959.

Despite initially rejecting the position, Fidel Castro eventually became president and implemented a series of popular social reforms and policies. The goal was to nationalize most foreign and Cuban owned land and businesses, in order to return wealth to the Cuban people. While the United States was initially willing to recognize the Castro government, it later chose not to do so, out of fear that the legitimization might cause a spread of socialist uprisings throughout Latin America. At the same time, most Cubans still resented the American government for its earlier support of Batista's regime. After the Castro government nationalized all American owned property on the island, the US government retaliated by freezing all Cuban assets on American soil, severing diplomatic ties and implementing a sweeping embargo against all exports to Cuba.

Following the American embargo, the Soviet Union became Cuba's main ally. Strong political and economic ties developed. Cuba received a great deal of economic support from the Soviet Union, enabling Castro's social revolution to proceed unhindered. Despite the communist inspired government, Cuba developed a relatively high degree of wealth, and income disparity was greatly reduced. Free education and healthcare was a tenet of the revolution and greatly increased the social and economic standings of even the poorest citizens.

Upon the collapse of the Soviet Union in 1991, foreign aid was greatly limited and Cuba experienced a severe depression, which Cubans refer to as *El Período Especial* (The Special Period). The country lost approximately 80% of its imports, 80% of its exports and its Gross Domestic Product dropped by 34 percent. Famine and malnutrition was high, forcing the government to enact a radical series of reforms to offer daily food rations and use tourism to boost the economy. Throughout Cuba, old hotels were remodeled and new hotels were built, as infrastructure was created to accommodate international tourists. Tourism, which had previously been a minor economic driver, had become, by the late 1990's, the island's main source of revenue.

The Special Period is generally recognized as having ended at about the year 2000. The fostering of close relations with Venezuela, after the election of socialist president Hugo Chavez in 1998, had a major positive impact on Cuba's economy. The countries forged a close alliance in order to further their shared political and economic goals. Today, many of the young people in Cuba have little first hand knowledge of The Special Period, and negative views towards the United States have greatly subsided. Evidence of past policies to deal with the economic hardship are still present, but Cuba has made significant headway in becoming a diversified, industrial nation, albeit with a communist/socialist structure. The American embargo still persists and is one of the largest points of contention between the two nations. Fidel Castro ceded political control to his brother Raul in 2008, but was still considered to be the ideological leader of the country. Fidel Castro died on November 25, 2016, at the age of 90.

Economics

Cuba has a socialist, state-controlled economy. Fundamentally, this means that the government controls almost all the basic means of production and employs the majority of the labor force. In recent years reforms have been implemented in order to foster small, independent enterprise.

While the average Cuban does not have a lot of money, the state does provide for everyone equally and basic needs are supplied to all citizens. The average monthly salary is often stated as being approximately $30 per month, but this does not take into account the host of free services and products provided by the government. Healthcare is free. Food staples are distributed freely, with additional portions available at a nominal cost. Education is free. Government jobs are provided to virtually anybody who wants to work. Utility bills such as telephone, electricity and gas are all extremely cheap because of government subsidization. While money is still necessary, it is perfectly possible to live comfortably with very little. Despite this fact, most Cubans are hard working and take great pride in their personal and collective achievements.

Although still technically communist, the government has implemented a series of progressive economic reforms in order to expand the private sector of the economy. Most types of small business are permitted and private ownership and transaction in real estate and vehicles is permissible. Many regulations still harken back to communist policies, but capitalism is a growing trend, especially in the large cities, and its growth is progressing relatively unimpeded.

Society

The average Cuban, whether young or old, is remarkably similar to the average person anywhere else in the world. Young people spend their days in school, and afterward enjoy going to the movies, playing sports or working part time jobs. Adults spend their days working and then return home to cook and tend to domestic affairs. Evenings are spent watching television and socializing with friends and family. Weekends are used to relax and to work on personal projects. For people living in a large city, such as Havana, life will sometimes be more hectic and perhaps exciting. For Cubans living in more rural areas, farming is still a main priority.

While sometimes portrayed as a strict authoritarian society, the truth is that most laws and regulations in Cuba are remarkably similar to the rules in any western country. As a general rule, it is fair to assume that, if something is permitted in your home country, then it will most likely also be permissible in Cuba. The inverse is also generally true for illegal activities. Details will be provided later in this guide.

Education

Education is considered a right in Cuba and is provided free to all citizens. Primary school and high school are compulsory. After high school, students can continue their education in a college setting or learn a trade. In both cases, they can afterwards continue their education in a university at no cost. University usually lasts 5 years.

Continuing education courses are also offered to citizens after they have completed their formal educations. These range from language courses to professional certifications and trade schools. These courses are usually completely free or offered at only a nominal cost.

Interesting Fact: After graduating from university, most students are offered government jobs in their field of study. They are expected to work at these jobs for at least 2 years. This period is called *Servicio Social* (Social Service). After completing this time, they are free to change profession, work independently or go back to school.

Culture

Fundamentally, the tenets of Cuban culture are sharing and community involvement towards accomplishing common goals. This sentiment is not simply the result of propaganda; it does actually have deep-seated significance within the Cuban society. The country is literally an island, and, for the majority of its history, Cuba was simply a far flung Spanish colony whose inhabitants were both disenfranchised and left to fend for themselves. Cubans were forced to rally around these cooperative themes and rely on themselves for every need.

Even after the Cuban revolution, the culture still retained its backbone of community spirit. In many ways, the fact that the country has been under communist government control for the last half decade has actually helped to develop and preserve the fundamental identity of Cuba. Whereas the most pressing concern in most developed countries is career furtherance and money, Cubans as a whole, have been able to continue focusing on communal progression and social development.

At the same time, the community spirit which thrives on the island can sometimes make foreigners feel alienated. Some Cubans, especially those from rural areas, still retain a sense of distrust or apprehension towards foreigners. This is not primarily due to fear, but rather inexperience. In a large city like Havana, which sees many tourists each year, most locals are warm and welcoming. As integration and interaction with foreigners increases, the icy Cuban facade is melting.

Dancing is one of the most popular Cuban activities. Salsa dance and music thrive throughout the island, and it seems like almost everyone, young or old can suavely sway to a good beat. There is also a strong prevalence of formally trained ballerinas and musicians.

Music is also incredibly popular. It can often be heard blaring out of apartment and car windows from morning until night. All genres are represented, from traditional Cuban music, often referred to as *son*, to faster paced salsa, rumba and reggaeton. Songs often revolve around the subjects of poverty, country or city lifestyle, and love. Rock and roll music is also very popular and especially from older bands such as the Beatles and the Rolling Stones.

Art is another point of significance. Whether it be painting, wood carving, craft making, sewing, photography, singing, acting or writing, the average Cuban likely has at least one artistic talent and is not shy at all to show it off.

The intricate aspects of any culture are very difficult to summarize, but as you continue reading this guide, you will gain a good understanding of the Cuban identity.

One particularly fascinating concept of Cuban culture is the idea of self-sufficiency. In most western societies, claiming or striving to be self-sufficient is seen as a desirable quality. In Cuban society, it is often viewed as a negative character trait. Cubans refer to self-sufficiency in Spanish as *autosuficiente*. But rather than simply implying independence, the word connotes overconfidence, egoism and even arrogance. In Cuba, most people are accustomed to relying on others, and consider progress to be something which is accomplished by a community, rather than an individual alone. Too much independence, on a personal level, is seen as strange and counter-cultural.

Religion

After the revolution, religious practice was greatly restricted in Cuba. Officially the Cuban government adopted a policy of promoting atheism. Over 80% of the island's Catholic priests and Protestant ministers eventually left Cuba and the attendance of mass and participation in other religious activities almost evaporated. By the 1990's Cuban society had become almost completely secularized.

Nonetheless, there remained a very small group of devoted followers and after the fall of the Soviet Union, as restrictions against religion were lessened, the number of people identifying themselves as religious believers began to expand. As of 2013, the government recognizes the right of citizens to profess and practice any religious belief. Attendance and participation in religious activities is still extremely low, but there is a movement towards people identifying themselves as belonging to particular religious affiliations.

Hard statistics are difficult to come by, but it is estimated that the largest religious affiliation on the island is Roman Catholicism. There is also a high prevalence of West African religious practitioners, particularly for the religions of *Santeria* and *Yoruba*. These are commonly referred to as syncretic religions, as they are based on a mix of Christianity and West African beliefs, as well as inspirations from other religions.

Protestantism, Judaism and the Jehovah's Witness movement also have a small presence in Cuba.

Interesting Note: On occasion you will see men and women walking around Cuba wearing completely white clothing. Sometimes they are even holding a white sun umbrella or wearing a white head scarf. These are practitioners of the Santeria religion and they are wearing white as part of their initiation process of becoming Santeria priests or priestesses. They must wear white for one full year and limit their contact with people who have not been initiated into the religion.

Languages

Spanish is the main language spoken in Cuba. While in hotels and other major tourist locations the Spanish will be spoken eloquently and clearly, in most other settings the locals will speak a fast and dialected *Cuban* Spanish that may require some getting used to, especially if you are not perfectly proficient in the language. Cubans have a tendency to drop the "*s*" from the end of words and to speak very rapidly. Sometimes this can lead to a bit of confusion. In most cases, if it appears that you do not understand something, the Cuban speaker will gladly repeat it slowly and with added emphasis.

Italian and French are very popular second languages, especially for those Cubans living in large cities. Italy and France both have strong economic and touristic relations to Cuba, and French-speaking Canadians make up one of the largest tourist groups to visit the island, so it is no surprise that locals choose to learn those languages. Furthermore, the country of France offers low cost French language courses through a series of schools located in Cuba.

Russian is also spoken by many Cubans. This can be attributed to the fact that, due to the strong ties between the two countries in the 1970's and 80's, many Cubans attended university in the former

USSR, especially those studying science and technology.

English is taught to all Cuban students, however most do not speak it with proficiency. Outside of inadequate classroom lectures, there is little opportunity for young people to practice on a consistent basis. American television programs are broadcast on a local station, sometimes with English subtitles, and this can be useful to some Cubans interested in learning. Furthermore, American music is popular on the island. Despite this, fluent English speakers are uncommon, outside of tourist locations.

It is highly advisable to learn at least a few words of Spanish before coming to Cuba, if you want to be free to explore every aspect of the island from a non-tourist perspective. Knowledge of French, Italian or any other Latin language will be a major asset. If you have no knowledge of Spanish and no time to learn before your visit, your best bet might be to make friends with a local Cuban who speaks English, as this will open many doors for you to immerse yourself in the local culture.

In tourist hot spots such as resorts, popular restaurants and hotels in most large cities, the staff will usually speak English, as well as some French, Italian, German, and even Russian. Lack of Spanish skills is one of the main reasons foreigners are hesitant to roam far from tourist spots. However, I have found most Cubans to be extremely helpful and capable of communicating even complicated matters despite a language barrier. As such, language difficulties should never be a very large concern on the island or keep you from experiencing everything it has to offer.

Some Common Cuban Slang

Almendron: old American car
Baro: money
Bici: bicycle
Bici-taxi: bicycle taxi

Bodega: state owned grocery store
Blumer: women's underpants
Bisnero: business man
Campesino: farmer
Camello: city bus
Carro: car
Carnet: Cuban identity card
Chancletas: flip-flops
Chao: goodbye
Chica: girl
Chopin: shopping
Cola: lineup or queue
Cuarto: a room in a hotel or house
Espejuelos: glasses
Fosforera: lighter
Frigi: refrigerator
Guayabera: official Cuban formal shirt
Jeva: woman
Jinetera: escort girl
Jinetero: male broker or vendor (gray market)
Máquina: old American car
Pinchar: to work
Pullover: T-shirt
Tenis: sneakers, sports shoes
Yuma: foreigner

Living Situations

Living situations in Cuba are different from those in most other countries. It is very common for several families to share a home or apartment, and dwellings are usually passed down from one generation to another. Privacy is highly prized, but very rare. It is common for adult children to sleep in the same room as parents, with nothing more than a curtain separating the beds. It is generally accepted that there is a large housing shortage in Cuba, especially in major cities like Havana.

It is also very common to see houses which are only half built or others which seem to be under construction for years. These house skeletons are sometimes boarded up with wood or plastic tarps and used as-is on a semi-temporary basis. Economic conditions are stressed, and despite labor being relatively cheap, it can still be very difficult for the average Cuban to put together enough money to start a construction project, and to actually finance it to completion.

House Exchanges

When situations necessitate a change of home, most houses are traded or exchanged rather than being bought or sold. This exchange of living quarters is called *permutar*. Cubans post signs on their homes or on communal bulletin boards, advertising that they would like to exchange their home for another one. For example, a large home in the city can sometimes be exchanged for two smaller apartments in the suburbs. Or a second floor apartment with a view can be exchanged for a similar first floor apartment with a parking space.

This process became necessary because up until a few years ago the buying and selling of homes was not legal. This was due to a law enacted by the government, shortly after the revolution, designed to make it impossible for one individual to own more than one home. The goal was to foster equality and limit the development of a wealthy landlord class. Under the *permutar* system, once an agreement has been reached, a notary takes care of the title transfers and the new titles are recorded with city officials. In all deals, there must always be an exchange of homes, although sometimes money also changes hands in order to make the deal fair.

Interesting Fact: Home-ownership was a tenet of the revolution. When the Castro government came into power, all private homes were nationalized, and title was given over to the dwelling occupants. Overnight, renters became homeowners. Landlords ultimately lost dearly as almost all of their property was released to the tenants.

Buying And Selling Property

In 2012, the Cuban government legalized the buying and selling of property on the island. For the first time since the revolution, Cubans could sell their home or buy a new one. Owning more than one home is currently permitted, with some restrictions. This was seen as one of the first steps for the government to move away from a hard-line, state-controlled economy to one of a public/private partnership of sorts, with increased private enterprise.

The real estate industry is still nascent and transaction volumes are low. Home prices are far higher than the wealth that most Cubans can ever expect to accumulate in a lifetime. Apartments in some large cities can easily have asking prices equating to over $50 000 USD, making their acquisition nothing more than a dream for the average worker. Most transactions are conducted by Cubans who have access to foreign financial sources, such as family members who live outside of the country.

It is important to note that real estate transactions are only permitted between Cuban citizens. Foreigners are not permitted to own or purchase property on the island.

Interesting Fact: In the past, if a Cuban citizen was to leave the island and seek exile in a foreign country, such as the United States, he or she would forfeit all property owned in Cuba. This property, including the home and all its contents would be repossessed by the state. This is no longer the case. Citizens are now permitted to retain all their belongings on the island even after they seek exile in a foreign country. They are also permitted to retain their Cuban citizenship and to freely re-enter the country.

Small Business

As mentioned earlier, over the last years, the Cuban government has initiated plans for economic reform aimed at reducing the size of the government payroll by stimulating small business development. It is now estimated that there are over 400 000 independent small business owners in Cuba. This is still a very small number compared to the island's total population of over 11 million inhabitants, but it is a clear sign that the government is serious about the initiative and that there is a desire from Cubans to establish themselves as independent business owners rather than relying on the state for all their economic needs.

In Cuba's larger cities, small businesses are everywhere. Walking down a street crowded with independent vendors operating out of doorway storefronts and small curbside stalls, you would be forgiven for thinking that communism was nothing more than a footnote in the country's history books. Capitalism is clearly making headway here and the list of permissible independent business types seems to be expanding on a monthly basis. The following list describes some of the most common independent businesses permitted in Cuba.

Restaurant and Fast Food: Even before it was legal, the independent restaurant industry was always a popular way for Cubans to make a bit of extra money. In the past, Cubans would operate clandestine restaurants out of their houses. Nowadays, they are permitted to open and operate restaurants and fast food stands and this has become one of the most profitable independent forms of employment. These restaurants are officially referred to as *paladares*. They range from the tiniest street side stand, selling fresh baked donuts, to the largest, fanciest, full scale, sit down locations, located in expensive tourist hot spots.

Household Items Vendor: These vendors can sell almost any household item, provided that it is made in Cuba. These items include pottery, cooking utensils, pipe fittings, gaskets and rubber washers as well as a host of blender and coffee-maker parts.

Music Disc Sellers: These vendors sell a variety of bootlegged CD's with crudely printed cover art. Prices are cheap, with most albums selling for the equivalent of $1USD or less. If you are walking down the street and hear loud reggeton or salsa music, it's a good sign that one of these vendors is somewhere near.

Artisanal Clothing Sellers: In Cuba, the word artisanal is used to describe hand-made items, manufactured within Cuba. This can range from clothing sewn by an independent seamstress, to shoes manufactured in a larger scale Cuban shoe factory. In previous years, clothing sellers exploited a loophole in the law and started selling imported clothing and shoes. This soon grew to be a large market and negatively impacted the domestic manufacturing industry. In 2014, most selling of imported goods by independent vendors was prohibited. These vendors now sell exclusively Cuban made products. A black market for foreign items does exist and vendors usually sell their outlawed, imported goods from the back of their stores, or through clandestine, door to door sales.

Independent Services: The service industry in the country is experiencing huge growth as well. Due to the American trade embargo and the low, average Cuban income, the maintenance, repair and repurposing of old products has long been a cornerstone of Cuban culture. Nowhere is this better exemplified than by the huge number of independent watch, mobile phone, and computer repair shops, as well as the throngs of jewelers, locksmiths and eyeglass technicians. Many of these services used to be offered exclusively by the state, but it seems that the general consensus is that independent workers can often do the jobs better, more quickly and at almost the same price. Print shops and photocopy centers are also seeing huge growth.

Collective Farming: In rural areas of the country, where economic opportunities are tighter, there has been a surge of independent farmers banding together into co-ops, in order to better set viable prices for their produce, and to reduce costs. They are taking advantage of government programs aimed at deregulating the farming and produce distribution industries. Whereas these farmers were once employed by the government and worked exclusively on state-run farms, they are now free to work their own fields and sell their crops wherever they want, at the best price possible. Many

Cubans see this as one of the greatest signs of the growing capitalist movement within the country.

Cubans Traveling Abroad

Cubans have always been permitted to travel abroad, but they were required to seek special government permission to do so. This permission was almost always denied. This established a *Catch-22* situation in which travel was technically legal, but practically impossible. In recent years, travel restrictions have been greatly relaxed. Cubans are now permitted to visit other countries, provided that they have a valid reason for travel and an appropriate foreign visitor visa from the host country (often the most difficult document to obtain). The high cost of travel has still largely kept this new found opportunity out of the hands of the average Cuban.

Many foreign-based organizations operate throughout the island with the goal of making travel dreams become a reality. Usually these organizations are run by foreign governments, especially from Europe and South American, offering short, all expense paid trips outside of the country, as educational, cultural, or language exchanges. Applications for these trips are high and acceptance rates are very low. Applicants are usually young adults, under the age of 25. For many Cubans, these exchanges are seemingly the best, or sometimes the only, opportunity they will have to travel abroad and experience life in another country, if only for a week or two.

Cuban Exiles

Undoubtedly, you have heard the stories of Cuban citizens using boats or hand made rafts to flee the island under the cover of darkness. This was a major problem in the past, but since the end of the *Special Period*, the prevalence of this activity has decreased. Despite being an extremely dangerous act, it is estimated that about 10 000 to 15 000 Cuban citizens, especially the poorer ones, or those with pressing needs, choose this option to flee the island, each year.

The Cuban word to describe exiles who have clandestinely left the country by boat is *balseros*. This is a term derived from the Spanish word for raft, which is *balsa*. Most modern Cubans no longer recognize it to be a realistic option for emigrating from the island, nor do they acknowledge the need for it under the present situation. Many young people joke about it as an act of exaggerated desperation.

The Cuban government has programs in place and multinational agreements which enable Cubans to safely and legally emigrate. Every year the United States issues over 20,000 visas which permit Cubans to legally leave the island and immigrate to America. The number of legal visas granted under the program is still small compared to the demand, but it is a viable option for the majority of people who want to leave for the purpose of family reunification or marriage.

Interesting Fact: Contrary to popular belief, attempting to leave the country in order to seek exile in a foreign nation was never seen as a very serious offense by Cuban law enforcement. The majority of Cubans who attempt to flee and are unsuccessful in reaching their destination are simply returned to Cuba where they are permitted to continue living their lives, without any incarceration or punishment. On the other hand, the brokers and speed boat operators who attempt to profit by trafficking exiles and smuggling Cubans to America are treated more severely. Their enterprise is seen as unscrupulous and dangerous to the lives of all boat occupants and punishments are harsh.

Police and Law Enforcement

There is a strong police presence in Cuba, especially in the major cities, but these officers almost never interfere in the daily lives of most Cubans. It seems that most of these law enforcement officials spend the majority of their day simply chatting amongst themselves on street corners. Despite the common perception that communist/socialist governments operate with a heavy hand, the power of law enforcement on the island seems to be pretty muted.

Although the average Cuban is leery of the police, there is a common understanding that unless you are doing something which overtly transgresses the law in a very bad way, the police will not get involved. In all my years of travel throughout the island, frequently taking me through some of the seediest looking areas, I have only seen police detain one person, and it was a rather calm event, seemingly stemming from a suspicion of a petty theft.

Far and away the major work of police is in traffic law enforcement. It is very common to see officers perched at street corners throughout the city and especially on highways, stopping drivers on the suspicion of speeding, drunk driving and usually just to check vehicle documentation and taxi driver certificates. Fines for minor infractions are small and are usually paid on the spot.

The police force in Havana is mostly composed of men and women who are not native to the city. Most officers are originally from the poorer eastern provinces and are relocated to work in Havana. The officers are paid above average wages and are given a house or apartment in Havana upon their relocation. The ranks are composed almost equally of men and women.

Interesting Fact: Inter-provincial immigration within Cuba is strictly regulated. In order for citizens to move to another province they must have a good reason for doing so, such as for school, work or important family commitments. This law serves to prevent a population exodus from the poorer eastern provinces into the richer, western provinces. More specifically, it prevents a mass migration to the country's richest city, Havana. Many young men and women from the eastern provinces join the police force precisely for the opportunity to immigrate to Havana. There is very little desire from Havana locals (Habaneros) to become police, because there are so many other economic opportunities in the city.

Important Laws to Remember

Drugs

Cuba has a zero tolerance policy towards drug possession, selling, usage, cultivation and importation. This applies to all illegal drugs, including marijuana. If you are caught with drugs, there is a very high probability that you will spend a while in prison. The police take this matter very seriously and they have drug sniffing dogs present at all airports and points of entry. At large political rallies and social gatherings such as concerts, sports events and street fairs, it is also very common to see drug sniffing dogs.

The use of drugs, even soft-core ones such as marijuana, is extremely low in Cuba. It is safe to assume that the great majority of the people you meet have never experimented with any of these substances and are not even familiar with their effects. This is in stark contrast to many other developed nations in the word.

This is not to say that drugs cannot be found in Cuba. While local drug use if low, there are ample opportunities for foreigners to purchase soft-core and hardcore drugs. These drugs are usually very expensive and not likely to be of very high quality. I strongly suggest that you come to Cuba to experience everything beautiful the island has to offer while staying away from anything drug-related.

Alcohol and Smoking

It is perfectly legal to drink alcohol openly throughout Cuba, except while driving a motorized vehicle. There is no legal drinking age, but it is illegal to sell alcohol to anyone less than 18 years of age.

Drinking and driving is considered to be a serious offense in Cuba, and should be avoided both for legal and safety reasons. Drinking and driving amongst Cubans is rare, as cars are extremely expensive and are very costly to repair. From a financial standpoint, it's just not worth the risk.

Smoking is completely legal outdoors and on restaurant terraces. It is very common for office workers to smoke inside government buildings. Smoking is legal in most bars, discos and hotels although it is becoming increasing popular to post no smoking signs in restaurants. It's safe to say that unless there is a no smoking sign posted, you are free to light up.

Sex

The age of consent between a foreigner and a local Cuban is 18. Any sexual contact between a foreigner over the age of 18 and a local under the age of 18 is considered illegal, and is punishable by prison time.

All other forms of sexual relationships are both completely legal and socially acceptable. There are very few taboos in Cuba. Schools teach safe sex practices ad-nauseam, starting at a very young age. Condom use in Cuba is among the highest in the industrialized world and sexually transmitted disease rates are among the lowest globally. Almost all state-run stores sell condoms, and many organizations give them away for free. Foreigners can buy condoms at state-run cafeterias, restaurant bars, fast food locations and pharmacies (farmácias). The cost is only 1 peso for a pack of 3.

Interesting Note: In Cuba, the tourist is king. In a dispute between a Cuban citizen and a foreigner, police will almost always take the side of the tourist. Although this gives foreigners a distinct upper hand in any argument, it is a privilege that should obviously not be abused. Common sense should always be exercised, and, generally, if something is illegal in your country of origin, it is fair to assume that the same act is illegal in Cuba. If you commit a serious crime, regardless of where you come from, you will be prosecuted.

Jineterismo

Jineteras and *jineteros:* You will hear these terms a lot in Cuba. Over the last 20 years, they have become part of the culture of the country. A thorough explanation of the subtleties of their meanings would be very lengthy. I will present a brief overview. For more details you can browse the internet or simply ask a local Cuban.

The word *jinetero* roughly translates in English to "jockey." Fundamentally, jineteros are Cubans who earn a living or glean extra money from tourists through illegal or semi-legal economic activity. While many tourists will simply lump everything together and refer to these Cubans as prostitutes, that generalization is misleading and often inaccurate. While prostitution can be a part of the equation, it often is not.

Jineteros can be men who approach tourists to sell cigars, liquor, drugs, counterfeit or stolen goods, or facilitate the brokering of sexual services. In addition they can broker taxi and other transportation services or help tourists find accommodations. Cubans who work independently, selling souvenirs, or who spend their day soliciting money, clothes, or other items from tourists are also generally referred to as jineteros. As you can see, while the term can refer to the selling or brokering of sex, it does not specifically mean that these individuals are prostitutes or pimps, or that sex is a main part of their business.

The term *jinetera* is generally reserved specifically for a woman who is a prostitute or earns money by providing some sort of escorting service. This can sometimes only involve accompaniment and not actual sex. Unlike in western culture, there is not a huge stigma attached to female sex workers in Cuba.

Contrary to what some people may claim, jineteros are not all hustlers, gangsters or violent criminals. Often they are simply regular citizens who are in desperate need of money and turn to shady practices in its pursuit. While some people consider

31

jineterismo a sign of the degradation of core Cuban values, others point out that gray or black market businesspeople are present in all societies and in Cuba, especially, their development was spurred by poor economic conditions which forced many to enter this line of work in order to survive. Due to government crackdowns in the last few years, and Cuba's improving economy, there has been a significant drop in jinetero and jinetera activity although you are still likely to encounter it in tourist-heavy areas.

Old Cars

No doubt you have seen postcards, photos and videos of old American cars still operating throughout Cuba. This is not a myth. Antique American and Russian vehicles dominate the traffic on the streets throughout the country. The classic American cars are relics of a time before the revolution when economic relations between Cuba and America were close. After the revolution and subsequent trade embargo, Cuba was thrown into economic disorder and the population was forced by necessity to continue using and maintaining these antiquated vehicles, having limited means to purchase newer ones.

The old, American vehicles are colloquially known in Cuba as *Chebi*'s, owing to the popular Chevy brand. They are also referred to as *maquinas* or *almendrons* (because of their large, almond shaped bodies). However, while these cars look original superficially, under the hood they have been greatly modified. The original gasoline engines were all replaced with diesel engines in the late 90's in order to reduce fuel costs and increase efficiency. As a consequence, they now rumble around the city, creating much more noise than they did originally, and often leaving a dark trail of smoke in their path. Most drivers of these old vehicles buy low cost heating oil type fuels through a black market network rather than buying official diesel fuel at state prices.

The next most popular vehicles are Russian Lada and Moskvich brand cars, characterized by their signature boxy look and delicate features. These were imported throughout the 70's and 80's as relations between Russia and Cuba solidified.

Currently, Cuba has fostered close relations with China and the prevalence of modern looking vehicles under popular Chinese brands such as Cherry and Geely is increasing. These cars are especially common in the rental car market. It is also not so unusual to see expensive European sports cars and luxury vehicles driving around, especially in large cities. These vehicles are usually imported by foreign embassies that have staff conducting business on the island.

Interesting Fact: Any motorized vehicle, no matter the age or type, is considered a prized possession in Cuba. Old vehicles from the 1960's are commonly listed for sale for tens of thousands of dollars. The reason these vehicles are worth so much is because of the income potential they can provide as taxis. While the average state job might pay no more than $30 per month, a taxi driver can potentially make $30 per day, if he owns and operates his own vehicle. This would equate to about $10 000 per year, an almost unheard of sum of wealth in Cuba. All cars are cherished and rigorously cared for, passed down from one generation to another, usually sustaining the livelihood of several families.

C.D.R. (Comités de Defensa de la Revolución)

Walking around anywhere in Cuba or Havana you will undoubtedly see doorways or billboards inscribed with the letters CDR, with perhaps a short slogan or number written below. These signs are so common that you might become oblivious to them. In fact, they symbolize one of the most enduring and controversial links to the communist revolution on the island.

The CDR system was created by Fidel Castro in 1960. The idea was for each neighborhood, throughout Cuba, to have a committee of local residents, overseeing the progress of the revolution. These Committees for the Defense of the Revolution would meet regularly to discuss local issues, organize activities to promote the revolution and provide a forum for residents to express themselves.

Detractors of the system contend that it is nothing more than an organization which monitors and spies on the population, while usurping individual freedoms and fostering mistrust within communities.

Proponents of the system often concede that the reputation of the CDRs has been tarnished by repressive acts committed by members, in the past. But, currently, the system's pros far outweigh the cons. Not only do CDRs provide a feedback loop for the government and regular citizens, but they serve to promote medical and educational campaigns, and have been effective at fighting and preventing corruption.

In practice, for most Cubans, participation in CDR meetings is rather limited. For large events, such as the May 1st, International Workers Day rallies, the local CDR presidents and active members will make great efforts to get as many people as possible from the neighborhood to attend and participate in the festivities. For many residents, given busy work and social lives, that might be the only CDR event they attend all year.

General Cuba Tourist Information

Cuban Currency

In order to make any purchases in Cuba, you must use Cuban currency. There are two types of currency in Cuba. The *convertible peso* (Peso Convertible) and the *Cuban peso* (Moneda Nacional). It sounds complicated, but it is not.

Contrary to some popular myths, foreigners cannot buy goods using American dollars. This might have been the case at some point in the past, but it is no longer an option.

The Convertible Peso

Cuban Convertible Pesos (CUC)

The convertible peso is traded at the same value as the American dollar. It is typically referred to as the CUC (pronounced like the

English word *cook*). It is the currency that most foreigners use in Cuba. It has a high buying power and is the only form of currency accepted at hotels and large state-run stores. The CUC can be broken down into 100 *centavos* (cents).

Since the CUC is pegged at a 1 for 1 rate to the American dollar, all you have to do to calculate the exchange rate for your money to CUC is to calculate the exchange rate of your native currency to the American dollar.

Note: If you are exchanging American dollars to CUC, there is an additional 10% tax for the conversion, meaning that your American dollars will only get 90% of their converted value. For that reason, it is always more economical to use Canadian currency or Euros when converting to CUC.

The Cuban Peso

Cuban Moneda Nacional Pesos (MN)

The Cuban peso is usually referred to as the *Moneda Nacional*. Its name is commonly abbreviated as *CUP* or *MN*. It was the historical currency used in the country and its purchasing power has been highly eroded over the years. Most state workers are still paid in Moneda Nacional and the majority of Cubans use this currency for most of their daily transactions.

1 CUC is equal to 24 pesos in Moneda Nacional (MN). Calculated the other way around, 1 peso (MN) equates to about 4 cents CUC (4 centavos).

Interesting Fact: The Cuban government has recently decided that it will eliminate the dual currency system. They plan to eventually merge the CUC and the Moneda Nacional into a single common currency. A time-line for this unification has not yet been established. In preparation for this merger, many state stores (restaurants in particular) have begun accepting payment for their offerings in either currency. The exchange rate which many of these locations offer is usually 1 CUC = 23 MN. This is slightly inferior to the 1:24 rate charged at CADECA exchange houses.

Currency Advice

Most tourist guides dismiss the importance of the Moneda Nacional currency and recommend that foreigners simply stick to using the CUC currency. If you are staying at an all inclusive resort or plan to spend all of your time in touristy areas, then this is fine. If, on the other hand, you are planning to explore the island or visit non-touristy areas, it will be much more economical to use the Moneda Nacional currency for most of your expenditures.

The CUC currency is used in tourist resorts, high end hotels, fancy restaurants and to rent apartments. Furthermore, it is used in large state-run supermarkets and stores and to take certain types of taxis. While in some situations, you must pay for your goods and services in CUC, there are many other instances where you can shop at locations which sell identical products, at a far lower price, in MN currency. This guide will tell you about many of these locations.

Note: Sometimes you will hear the word *peso* used. Locals use the term to refer to both CUC and MN. Any currency amount of *1* can be called a peso. If the currency is not specified, it is best to make certain before buying something. Just ask the vendor if he means 1 peso MN or 1 peso CUC.

Exchanging Money

Unlike other currencies, there is no international exchange market for Cuban money. You will only be able to buy and sell Cuban pesos in Cuba. There are several ways to exchange your foreign currency.

CADECAs

In Cuba, you can change money in state-operated exchange houses called *CADECA*s. These locations are usually clearly indicated on street signs and can be found in all cities and towns and at most airports and hotels. The CADECAs located in cities usually offer better foreign exchange rates than those at hotels and airports. It is advisable to exchange just a bit of money at the airport, upon entering the country. This will give you some purchasing power until you can locate a CADECA offering better rates.

CADECA offices will exchange all types of foreign currency. The most common currencies exchanged are Euros, British Pounds and Canadian and American dollars. You cannot convert all currencies in Cuba. For example, Australian dollars are not accepted. To exchange some currencies, you might have to visit a main CADECA office rather than a satellite branch.

A full list of all the currencies which are accepted for conversion as well as their daily conversion rates can be seen at http://www.bc.gob.cu/English/exchange_rate.asp

Foreign currencies are all converted first to Cuban Convertible Pesos (CUC). If you want Moneda Nacional, you can convert your CUC currency to MN on a 1:24 basis, as part of a separate transaction.

Contrary to some beliefs, tellers at CADECA offices are very honest when exchanging foreign currency. Scams at these locations are extremely rare. In order to exchange foreign currency you will be asked to provide a piece of ID, usually a passport, and your information will be entered into a computer. The clerk will count out your money, confirming the amount with you, and then give you a printed slip indicating how much Cuban currency you will receive back. The clerk will then count out the Cuban currency two times before passing it to you. You are free to take your time to recount the currency. Generally, clerks will refuse all tips so as to remain completely impartial in the transaction.

Note: It is best to convert your foreign currency to Cuban currency at several intervals throughout your trip rather than converting everything at once. If you find yourself with a lot of Cuban currency at the end of your trip and want to convert it back to your original foreign money there will be substantial foreign exchange charges. This might easily reduce the value of your currency by 5%. Furthermore, taking a large amount of Cuban currency out of the country is not permitted. A few dollars is fine, but if Cuban customs finds that you have many hundreds of dollars in CUC as you exit the country, it can be confiscated.

Banks

Another way to exchange foreign currency is to use a bank. There are several large bank brands operating in Cuba, and all are capable of exchanging foreign currency. Although banks might, on occasion, offer slightly better exchange rates than CADECAs, it should be noted that the lineups to get into a bank are often very long. In addition, while a bank can exchange your foreign currency into CUC, they are not permitted to exchange CUC into MN. The only place to do this is at a CADECA.

Other Foreigners

One of the cheapest ways to convert currency is to exchange it privately with other foreigners. This strategy works best for the most popular currencies like Canadian dollars, Euros, and American dollars. The best location to meet foreigners looking to exchange currency is at an airport CADECA. You will usually encounter many foreigners who have just completed their trip in Cuba and are eager to sell their leftover CUC. Since CADECAs usually charge an exchange fee of at least 5%, you can offer a slightly lower rate and buy these CUC directly from the foreigners. You will both benefit by saving the standard exchange fees.

Electronic Banking

Credit Cards

Credit card usage in Cuba is very rare. The only places that are equipped with credit card processing equipment are large tourist resorts, and hotels in main cities. Restaurants and state stores almost never accept credit cards.

If you are planning on bringing and using a credit card, make absolutely sure that it has not been issued from an American banking institution. All American-based credit cards will be refused because of the American embargo on trade with Cuba. Most other credit cards, especially those issued from European or Canadian banks can be used.

ATMs (cajeros automaticos) are rare. A few can be found in some hotels and very touristic areas in large cities, and at major airports. You should never depend on these machines. Breakdowns are frequent and withdrawal limits are low. In some cases, even if you are using a credit card issued from a non-American institution, you may still require the assistance of a bank teller in order to complete your transaction.

Personal checks, traveler's checks, and bank drafts are almost completely unheard of.

<u>PayPal And Other Payment Transfer Services</u>

It should be noted that due to the trade embargo, you will **not** be able to use any American based money transfer services while in Cuba. If these services are web based, such as PayPal, you will be able to access the websites; however the actual payment will be blocked. This applies even if you are paying for something which is completely unrelated to Cuba. Simply attempting to initiate a transfer via a computer based in Cuba may lead to the temporary suspension of your account. The American government enforces the trade embargo very vigilantly, especially when it comes to international money transfers.

<u>Note:</u> Despite the thawing of relations between the USA and Cuba and the resulting increase in American tourism to the island, as of early 2017 the trade embargo is still in place and financial transactions between the two countries are highly restricted. American based credit and debit cards will still not function in Cuba and the use of services like PayPal is not possible. American tourists are advised to bring enough cash to last the duration of their trip.

How Much Money to Bring

If you have prepaid your vacation and are staying at an all inclusive hotel, you will not need much money. You will mostly use cash to give tips or to buy small items and souvenirs. The only instance where you might need to spend more is if you decide to take a scenic excursion off the resort. That might cost the equivalent of a few hundred dollars, depending on the specifics of the trip.

If you are not staying on a resort, your expenses will obviously be higher. Detailed budgeting information is provided in the <u>Budgeting</u> section (p.143). In the most general sense, Cuban regulations state that foreigners must bring enough money into the country to reasonably last the duration of their stay on the island. This is highly subjective, but is usually understood to mean approximately the equivalent of $100 USD per day. For the average visit, this will be more than adequate. After reading this guide you will see that you can easily live like royalty, while only spending a fraction of that amount.

Potable Water

One of the most persistent worries I hear from prospective travelers to Cuba is that the water is unsafe to drink. On occasion, even local Cubans will warn travelers to only drink bottled water, as the tap water is of poor quality. Both of these claims are unsubstantiated. Save for a few very limited exceptions, the tap water on the island is perfectly safe and is of similar quality to tap water in most North American cities.

Cuba has a sophisticated network of desalination plants operating around the island as well as many extremely clean freshwater sources close to most large cities. Moreover, a cornerstone of the revolution was the promise to provide all citizens with clean, drinkable tap water. In any event, despite the fact that the tap water is perfectly safe, if you still have concerns, you can always simply buy bottled water in any Cuban supermarket at a very low cost. Water quality should never be used as an excuse to avoid visiting Cuba.

On occasion, as can happen in any city, a localized boil water advisement will be issued, usually due to construction work or a broken water main. This is rare and the advisement is issued usually as a precaution rather than a warning.

Interesting Note: There have, in the past, been a few, very limited, cholera outbreaks, usually affecting no more than half a dozen people, and always localized in the extremely poor outskirts of the far eastern provinces. These were proven to have been caused by poor sanitation within crowded living quarters rather than contaminated water sources. So, unless you anticipate sleeping on the floor of a crowded ghetto in a remote village located at the eastern tip of the island, you should have no worry at all about contracting cholera.

Transportation Options

Long distance Buses

The leading national bus service is called *Viazul*. It is safe, clean, cheap and very reliable. The bus routes cover the whole island and connect all the major cities. This is the most common way for tourists to get around the island and move from one city to another. The Viazul service uses a modern fleet of buses. Breakdowns and service interruptions are rare.

The most popular route is the Havana-Varadero link, as most tourists will at some point visit both of these cities and both cities offer international airports. Being located only 2 hours away from each other, it is common for tourists to arrive in Varadero and then simply take a bus to Havana, or vice versa. This will be discussed in more detail later on in this guide and a detailed bus schedule can be found in the section titled Getting to Havana Cheaply (p.96).

Astro Bus is another national bus line operator. It is similar to Viazul, however the fares are substantially lower, which often leads to extremely long waiting lists to reserve a ticket. It is next to impossible for foreigners to travel on Astro buses; for most practical purposes, Astro is reserved exclusively for Cuban citizens. Foreigners should avoid the hassle and potential boarding problems by simply using Viazul.

Taxis and Sharing Rides

For distances long and short, the use of taxis is very common throughout Cuba. Cities and small towns are inundated with taxi drivers eager to pull in a fare. But, while in most other countries taxis are used mostly for intra-city traveling, in Cuba it is also common to take a taxi on long distance trips.

Long Distance Taxis

The main bus terminals are very useful if you are looking to hire a car to get from one town to another. Around most terminals, taxi drivers and transport brokers will congregate and offer their services to all passersby. It can sometimes be a hectic scene, but when you are looking for fast and direct transportation to another city, this will be a great opportunity to find a cheap ride. While hiring a private taxi will usually be a bit more expensive than taking the bus, the cost can sometimes be lower, on a per capita basis, if you are traveling with several friends. If you are traveling alone and are seeking transport to a popular destination, you can negotiate an appropriate price with the taxi driver and then simply wait until other tourists or Cubans arrive, and speak with them about joining you, sharing the total trip cost.

Although the idea of meeting a taxi driver and then getting in a car with complete strangers on a long trip might seem daunting to some, in Cuba it is a safe and common occurrence. Because most vehicles in Cuba are old and the roads are heavily patrolled by police, drivers are very respectful of the speed limits. Just be mindful not to choose a taxi which looks too old, as breakdowns on the road are common and can lead to trip delays.

Local Taxis

There are two official forms of taxis in Cuba: State taxis and *Taxis Particulares (a*lso called **Taxis Colectivos)**

States taxis are usually painted yellow and black and have a taxi placard on the roof of the vehicle. These taxi vehicles are owned by the state and the fleet is mostly composed of boxy, Soviet-style cars

dating from the 1980's, or more modern Chinese or Korean brand vehicles. The taxis will pick you up and drop you off directly at your destination. They have a fare meter which can calculate the trip cost, but these meters are rarely used. In the vast majority of instances, the fares are negotiated before the trip. While prices vary according to your location, trip distance and negotiating ability, a general rule of thumb is to estimate about 1 CUC per kilometer of travel (for short-haul trips). Cross city trips usually cost less than 5 CUC. Always negotiate the fare beforehand so as to avoid unpleasant surprises. These taxis are plentiful in all large cities and it is usually not a problem to hail one from the side of the road by simply raising your arm into the street.

The other form of taxi in Cuba is the *Taxi Particular (*also called *Taxi Colectivo)*. These are officially licensed taxis which are operated out of privately owned, older model vehicles, usually dating from the 1960's or before. They have taxi placards in the window, but other than that, they are almost indistinguishable from other vehicles on the road. These taxis operate along a fixed route and will pick you up and drop you off at any point along that route, but will not bring you directly to a particular destination. These taxis are communal, and they usually hold 5 to 8 passengers, plus the driver. They basically operate like tiny buses. Next to walking and taking the bus, they are the most common form of transportation in Cuba. The cost to use these taxis is 10 pesos (MN), payable when you exit the taxi.

How to Hail a Taxi Particular

If you want to explore Cuba like a local and save a lot of money in transportation costs, you definitely have to learn how to use Taxis Particulares. The process of hailing one of these taxis is very simple. Just wait along the sidewalk of a main road leading in the general direction that you wish to travel. Extend your arm into the road and try to make eye contact with the passing drivers. Within moments a car will pull to the side and stop. Simply tell the driver the destination you desire or the neighborhood which you want to visit.

45

If your destination is close to his route, the driver will tell you to get in. If your routes do not match, the taxi will simply drive off without picking you up. It might take a little bit of practice at first, but eventually this will become your easiest and most economical form of transportation. The most difficult part is determining which main roads coincide with the routes that most of the taxi drivers use. The Havana taxi routes will be explained in great detail, in the Havana Taxi Particular Routes section (p.123).

<u>Sharing Rides on Unofficial Taxis</u>

Another general rule of thumb is that, in Cuba, almost anybody with a car, or other form of transportation for that matter, will be willing to give you a lift to your destination, for a bit of money, and sometimes, even for free. If you are in need of a ride and an official taxi is not available, you can almost always find an unofficial taxi anywhere on the island. Simply making eye contact with a driver or a person sitting beside a parked car will often be a conversation starter. With minimal negotiation, a deal can be arranged and you will be safely chauffeured to any destination.

The practice is extremely common and very safe. It's so common, in fact, that the locals have even created a term for it. *Coger la botella* is a phrase which translates to *"catch the bottle."* It means to get a free or very low cost ride. It's like hitchhiking, but there is no stigma or safety concerns about it in Cuba. In fact, Cubans often joke that hitchhiking is Cuba's national sport. Often, on early mornings and in the late afternoon, after school and work has ended, you will notice lines of men and women gathered around intersections and waiting along roadway medians. They chat with passing drivers and are able to get rides if the driver is going on the same route. Regardless of gender, beauty or age, this form of free transportation is open to everybody and is a testament to the culture of sharing and communal living which continues to be a hallmark of the Cuban revolution.

While it might be difficult for obvious foreigners to *catch* a free ride this way, it is certainly possible to use it as a low cost form of transportation when all else fails. In some cases, a conversation with a foreigner, to learn about different cultures and parts of the world, is the only payment requested by the driver.

Although these taxis are unofficial, they are usually very safe; but obviously use discretion whenever entering a vehicle. Contrary to what you might read on the internet, it is not illegal for a foreigner to take a ride in an unofficial taxi. While the driver can face stiff fines if he is caught operating as a taxi without a license, the tourist is not blamed. The practice is widespread and generally tolerated by the state.

City Buses

All major cities in Cuba have dedicated municipal buses. These are usually very cramped and overcrowded. The cost to use a city bus is 40 cents (MN) which is approximately 2 cents CUC. In larger towns the city buses are very similar to city buses used anywhere else in the world, although they tend to be a little bit older and more worn. There is no air conditioning.

City buses often travel unmarked or vaguely marked, and schedules are hugely unreliable. Stops can be indicated in a number of different ways, usually either by a covered bus stop shelter, or a small sign on the side of the road with a bus symbol and perhaps a bench. Routes, destinations and schedules are almost never marked. Even for many Cubans, taking the bus can be a hair-raising proposition.

Interesting Fact: During the 1990's Cuba suffered a transportation crisis. There was a great need for public transportation, but the government had little money to spend on purchasing buses. The Cuban government solved the problem by constructing rudimentary buses out of old machinery. Fundamentally, they used large tractor rigs to pull around passenger carts. These transports were colloquially called *camellos,* because their shape resembled the outline of a camel's dorsal humps. These are still used on a limited basis in some of the eastern provinces, but they are mostly obsolete, having been replaced by modern buses. Smaller, antique buses, dating from the 1950's are still common on the road in most cities during off peak hours. Many Cubans now colloquially refer to most city buses as *guaguas*, because of the chugging sound they make.

Private Buses

Yet another form of cheap transportation is the *Uso Particular* bus. These are basically buses operated by private individuals or companies. Cost can vary depending on the route, but prices are usually nominal by foreign standards. For routes within the city, the price is usually only 5 pesos (MN). You can get off at any point along the route. This kind of bus can come in any number of different shapes and sizes. In large cities, they often look like regular city buses that are painted yellow and black. In rural areas, these buses might simply be flat bed transport trucks, like the kind that would commonly be used to move produce, retrofitted with benches and guardrails. In either case, if they are independently owned and operated buses, they will always have the words *Uso Particular* painted on the side.

<u>Important Note:</u> In Cuba, the word *particular* usually refers to something which is private or independent. A *taxi particular* or a *uso particular* bus, simply means a private or independently owned bus or taxi. It is simply a way to distinguish these vehicles from the typical, state-owned buses or taxis. In the <u>Accommodation Options</u> section (p. 50) of this guide you will learn about *casas particulares*, which are basically just privately owned houses and rooms which you can rent out, as opposed to rooms in a state owned hotel.

Flights

Cuba has a well developed air travel network. Cubana Airlines is the country's national airline and also the largest operator of national and international routes. While there were some safety concerns revolving around Cubana in the past, over the last few decades it has dramatically improved performance by completely upgrading its airplane fleet and modernizing facilities. The airline's safety and performance is currently on par with all other North American operators. In fact, the majority of Cubana's airplanes are far newer than the average throughout the airline industry, and in terms of friendliness and comfort, Cubana is ranked well above the mean. If you were hesitant about taking flights in Cuba because you imagined boarding a rickety, propeller aircraft that was originally manufactured decades ago, you can rest assured, that is not the case.

For international flights, Cubana operates a fleet of new Airbus jets which usually travel at full capacity. For internal flights, they fly new Antonov regional passenger jets. Although Antonov does not have the name recognition of either Boeing or Airbus, it is, nonetheless, one of the largest aircraft manufacturers in the world with a high safety score. Aside from some small superficial differences, the Antonov jets look, feel and perform almost identically to Airbus and Boeing planes.

Flights can be purchased online, via the Cubana website (www.Cubana.cu) and are also available through tour operators. In Cuba, flights can be purchased at Cubana sales offices located in all major cities and towns. Flights purchased in an office, with cash, are usually a bit cheaper than those purchased online. Also, it is important to note that Cuban citizens can purchase flight tickets at dramatically reduced cost. For example, while a standard flight from Havana to Santiago de Cuba (located on the other tip of the island) can cost 150 CUC for a foreigner, a Cuban citizen will only pay about 12 CUC. If you are traveling with a Cuban companion, it is always cheaper to have them buy their own flight tickets directly at a Cubana sales office.

Accommodation Options

All inclusive Resorts

The great majority of tourists who visit Cuba stay at all-inclusive resorts. They are a good option for travelers looking to relax on the beach and experience a fun vacation where they don't have to think about day to day issues. These accommodation options do not offer much opportunity to experience the authentic Cuba. Most inclusive resorts are situated away from major cities, in specially built resort towns. Since the food, drink and entertainment is provided on the resorts, there is little reason for the average tourist to leave the resort campus and explore the surrounding area.

Considering that this guide is aimed at travelers who intend to experience the authentic Cuban culture, I will not go into great detail on the subject of all-inclusive resorts. I will, however, provide a brief overview of their main services, as their prevalence on the island and popularity with foreigners cannot be ignored. I will go into a bit more detail describing the resort town of Varadero, as it is located only a 2 hour drive away from Havana, and many visitors to Havana come as part of a day trip excursion from Varadero.

Varadero is the largest resort town in Cuba and the top tourist destination in the country. It offers accommodations for every age and price range. All-inclusive resort stays can be booked through a variety of websites and many airlines offer flights to Varadero along with package trip discounts. Often, the price of booking a travel package, which includes air travel and accommodations at an all-inclusive resort, will be only marginally higher than the price of booking a flight alone. This is another reason why most tourists choose to book all-inclusive package vacations.

Prices for all-inclusive packages vary considerably throughout the year. The low tourist season generally runs from May to September, but frequently, the best prices can be found on vacations occurring in early January or late November. By far the most expensive time to book a vacation is during the Canadian spring break, from mid February to mid March.

In order to get the most up to date information about a particular resort, I recommend researching the hotel on review websites like TripAdvisor.com. In many cases, there is a direct correlation between the price paid for the hotel and the quality. The commonly used "star" rating system is not directly applicable to most Cuban resorts. What might be called a 4-star resort in Varadero, might only translate to a 3-star Mexican resort. In general, a Cuban hotel rated at 3.5 to 4 stars will offer the most cost effective and comfortable experience. Anything rated below 2.5 stars will usually be disappointing and hotels of that caliber are frequently marketed as "Cuban" hotels rather than tourist resorts.

Standard Hotels

Standard hotels can be found in all cities and towns in Cuba. These are mostly, but not exclusively, frequented by foreigners. They are all state-run, and usually offer quality accommodations at a reasonable price.

The best place to look for and reserve a hotel in Cuba is online. You will be able to find photos and detailed reviews of almost every hotel in Cuba. In a large city like Havana, basic hotel rooms can be reserved for about 25 CUC per person, per night. Fancier hotels can be much more expensive, easily reaching 100 CUC per night or more. In Cuba, it is always cheaper to reserve hotel rooms online, rather than just showing up at the front desk. The savings will often amount to over 50%.

While hotels can be a good option for some tourists, there are some clear drawbacks. In terms of price, while a standard Cuban hotel is relatively cheap by western standards, it is still rather expensive. Furthermore, in a hotel setting you will always be surrounded by foreigners and your opportunities to interact with locals will be reduced. Most importantly, hotels will not permit visitors onto the premises unless they are paid guests at the hotel. If, for example, you make some local friends and want to host a small gathering in your hotel room, you will either have to sneak your guests into the room, or pay a full nightly fare for each visitor. This is a strict policy at all Cuban hotels.

If you are looking to save a lot of money and eager to completely immerse yourself in the local lifestyle and culture, there is a much better Cuban accommodation option, and it will be discussed in the next section.

Important Note: Contrary to common misconceptions, Cuban citizens *are* allowed to stay at all hotels on the island, provided they have a valid reservation and have paid the nightly fare. The hotel fare for a Cuban is exactly the same as that for a foreigner.

Casas Particulares

ARRENDADOR DIVISA

Throughout Cuba there is a highly developed private house and room rental network. These accommodations are called *Casas Particulares* (private homes). They offer some of the highest quality and lowest priced accommodations on the island. Moreover, since you will be staying inside an independently-owned dwelling with a Cuban landlord, you will have an opportunity to learn about the culture up close, from the vantage point of a regular citizen.

Casas particulares can be found throughout Cuba. Most are priced at about 20 CUC to 40 CUC per room, per night, although prices can go much higher for more luxurious accommodations. It is important to note that the casas are always rented on a per room basis, not on a per person basis. This means that, regardless if you are traveling solo or as a couple, you will always pay the same nightly rate.

Casas particulares are safe, cheap, and convenient. Their use and prevalence has increased dramatically in recent years. In most large Cuban cities, they have become the accommodation of choice for tourists.

All casas particulares must be licensed and undergo regular inspections by Cuban authorities to ensure that they meet the standards set by government regulations. In order for a Cuban to legally rent their house or a room in their house, they must pay a monthly tax to the state. Furthermore, the state has a list of basic necessities which must be provided whenever a dwelling is rented, such as a modern bathroom facility and a functioning air conditioner in each bedroom. Considering this, foreigners can expect a well maintained and functional dwelling whenever they stay at a casa particular. All licensed casas will always display a small, blue and white sign on the front door as shown in the image on the previous page.

There are three main types of casas particulares: completely independent, semi-private, and communal (hostel).

A completely private, or independent, house is one where you receive the keys to the main door and have full use of the house or apartment. This is a great option if you are looking for complete independence and privacy. If this is your desire, just be sure to rent a casa which only has one bedroom. If you rent a large casa which has several bedrooms, but you only pay to occupy one, then there is a possibility that the landlord might rent the other rooms to different guests, thereby impacting your privacy. All bedroom doors have their own locks, so in most cases, this is not a major issue. If you are traveling with friends, a common option is to rent a large apartment, with each person occupying a separate bedroom.

Another popular option is to stay in a semi-private casa. In this case you are simply renting a bedroom in a Cuban house. Usually this option is slightly cheaper than renting a completely private apartment. This option offers you the opportunity to interact more regularly with the Cuban homeowner and other people living in the house. Your bedroom will always be private, with its own locking door, but the general living quarters of the house, such as the living room, terrace and kitchen, will be shared. This casa rental option is commonly referred to as *Renta de Habitacion* meaning *Room Rental* in English. In certain cases, these semi-private casas might offer a small, private living area in addition to the private room. The house layout may be such that there is a semi-private apartment within the main home. Perhaps the only area of the house which is shared is the main front entrance.

The last type of casa particular is the hostel. Generally, these are large apartments or houses which are broken up into many different rooms or dorms, each rented out separately. As opposed to semi-private casas which might only have one or two rooms for rent, hostels might have dozens of rooms, with multiple beds per room.

Hostels in Cuba are usually very cheap, especially if you are traveling solo. If you are traveling as a couple or with friends, the relative difference in price as compared to the other casa particular options is minimal. While a hostel environment will offer you an opportunity to interact with foreigners from all over the world, your opportunity to interact on a familiar level with a Cuban host family, like you would have in a semi-private casa, will be reduced. In this guide I have not reviewed hostels in Cuba, but there is a lot of information available online.

General Casa Notes:

In almost all circumstances, Cuban citizens are allowed to accompany foreigners into casas particulares. Since the casa is rented by the night, and not by the person, no supplemental fees are required. The casa owner might require that Cuban guests sign a guest-book before being allowed entrance. In some cases, the guest will be asked to show identification. This is standard protocol and is done as a precaution, to reduce the risk of theft from the casa and for the foreigner's protection. If you rent a completely independent casa then this will not be an issue, as you will have your own front door key and can enter and leave in complete privacy, with whomever you want.

Most casas also offer low-priced dining options. Prepared breakfasts can often be had for about 3 to 5 CUC. Lunch and dinner prices are usually higher and vary according to the meal selected.

Upon arrival at a casa particular, the owners will ask for your visa. Your name and the details of your stay will be recorded in a registration book. Your signature will also be required. The house owner will take this information to be processed at a local immigration office and your visa should be returned within 24 hours.

If you are staying at a casa particular for an extended period of time, it is always advisable to pay in installments (for example, 4 nights at a time). This will ensure that if there are ever any problems with the casa, you can easily cut your stay short and find other accommodations.

You are never required to pay for your casa particular stay immediately upon arrival. Take a look around the casa and make sure you are satisfied with the condition of the unit. If you have not exchanged your foreign currency into Cuban currency, and it is already late in the evening, don't worry. You can relax for the night and just pay the next day, when you have had a chance to use a money exchange service.

For foreigners, all casa particular stays are priced in CUC currency. There are certain casas particulares which accept payment in Moneda Nacional, however, these are reserved for Cuban citizens only. As a foreigner, these will not be available to you. For your own knowledge, they are called *Arrendador Divisa* casas and they are indicated with a red and white casa particular sign, as opposed to a blue and white sign used for tourist casas.

Interesting Fact: It is usually best to negotiate prices and book your stay directly with the casa owner, rather than through a reservations broker. The broker will always charge a fee of 5 CUC per night to make a reservation, and this will inevitably be incorporated into your casa bill via a higher nightly room price. If you have a basic knowledge of Spanish you will be able to locate your own casa in most major Cuban cities simply by searching online Cuban classified pages such as Revolico.com.

BARGAIN BONUS ALERT!

Refer to The Real Havana: Cheap Casa Particular Guide at the end of this guide (p. 221) for a comprehensive selection of the highest quality and cheapest casas in Vedado. I have independently reviewed and stayed at each one of these casas.

Each casa particular mentioned in this book is part of the Real Havana network. Special, low rates have been negotiated with the landlords and all properties adhere to strict quality standards. Furthermore, when booking a stay at any of these casas, there are no middleman commissions to pay. This will potentially save you hundreds of dollars in brokerage fees.

More casa listings, as well as photos for all the casas listed in this guide, can be found on the website www.BestCubaGuide.com.

You can use this website to reserve the casas particulares directly, online, at no additional cost.

Dining Options

Resort Restaurants

If you are staying at an all inclusive resort, most of your dining will take place at the resort restaurants. In most resorts, the dining consists of a main buffet which operates at breakfast, lunch and dinner. There are also usually a few à la carte restaurants scattered around the main campus which operate at dinner time. Generally, the meal offerings at all the restaurants will be very similar. The main difference will be in the dining atmosphere. While the buffet might be crowded and noisy, the à la carte restaurants will tend to be quieter. The tradeoff is that there is no formal dress code at the buffet restaurants while the à la carte restaurants usually require diners to dress semi-formally. It is always best to check these details ahead of time with your particular hotel.

Regular Dining Options (outside of a resort)

Take note that the information regarding the quality of the food and service in these restaurants is highly subjective, and can change dramatically from one visit to the next. I try to focus mainly on the facts rather than to give opinions, unless I feel it is highly warranted.

There are four main types of dining establishments in Cuba: state-run restaurants, independent *paladares*, street-side, quick food establishments (colloquially named *Chiringos*), and state-run cafeterias and fast food locations.

State-Run Restaurants

These restaurants are exactly as the name suggests. They usually look and feel exactly like any western style restaurant, but they are not privately owned - they are state-operated and controlled. The majority of formal, sit down restaurants in Cuba are state-run. These establishments usually have a large staff, dressed in formal uniforms.

The restaurants usually have full alcohol permits and large menus. Furthermore, the restaurants often have prominently displayed names and are located near busy intersections and streets with high pedestrian traffic. They clearly look like large, professional restaurants.

Outside of a few restaurants located in very touristy areas, the majority of state-run restaurants are very reasonably priced and food quality is surprisingly good. Dining at restaurants has always been a large part of Cuban culture. Throughout the revolution, even during the Special Period, these restaurants offered the opportunity for Cuban citizens to experience a degree of relaxation and personal enjoyment without having to spend a lot of money.

It should be noted that the menu selection and prices are fairly similar at many of these state restaurants. Common menu items include pizza and pasta, along with a few meat or seafood offerings. Most entrées are priced at about 2 to 5 CUC. Most state restaurants will also offer special table d'hôte menus, generally referred to as *Ofertas*. These are always the most popular and cheapest meal options. They consist of a main dish, dessert and a drink. Portions are usually very generous and the total price for these complete meals is about 3 to 4 CUC. In the following section, titled Cuban Cuisine, I will outline the typical foods you can expect to order in these *Oferta* specials.

Most state-run restaurants in major cities have food prices marked in CUC. However, a fair number of restaurants can also be found which price their meals in Moneda Nacional. Prices at these restaurants are even more affordable and the service and food choices are almost exactly comparable to CUC priced restaurants.

Also, if you don't speak Spanish, you should know that the Spanish word for menu is *la carta.* If you are exploring the city and find an interesting restaurant, always ask to view *la carta* before entering, so that you can check out the menu and prices.

<u>Note:</u> The menus at all state-run restaurants will either be priced in CUC or MN. Sometimes the *food* will be priced in MN while the *drinks* (especially the alcohol) will be priced in CUC. This is normal. But, **there will never be** one menu for tourists, priced in CUC, and another for locals, priced in MN. Furthermore, the menu will always be typed out, never handwritten. I will elaborate on these points further in the section titled <u>Common Tourist Scams...</u> (p. 138).

<u>Paladares</u>

A *paladar* is a broad term used to describe any type of private restaurant in Cuba, from the largest and most formal private dining hall to the tiniest, street side fast food joint. For the purposes of this book, I will use the term paladar when referring to privately owned, sit down restaurants only.

Private restaurants are a very popular dining option for tourists throughout Cuba. They are usually a bit more expensive than state-run restaurants, although the food choices can be more varied. Many paladares will offer international dishes made from ingredients which they import. Some choose to focus on making authentic Cuban cuisine to the highest standards possible. The fact that paladares are privately owned usually means that the service and food quality will be higher than comparable state-operated establishments, but that is not always the case.

Generally, meals in a paladar will cost about 5 to 15 CUC per person. For more upscale choices, such as fish or lobster, you can expect to pay considerably more. Always review the details of your restaurant bill, as it is common to overcharge guests. Formal paladares almost always charge their fares in CUC, and if you do find one which advertises prices in MN, double check before you order, or you might have an unpleasant surprise at the end of the evening.

While some paladares are run out of large rented locations, the majority still operate from private homes which transform into intimate restaurants each evening. The locations of many formal, sit down paladares are not clearly marked on street level signage, so they can be difficult to find. These paladares generally rely on word of mouth advertising. On some occasions, they will hire people to stand in front of the restaurant or on busy street corners to solicit clients. There are specialized guidebooks which rate and list directions for individual paladar locations, and for the traveler who is particularly keen on going to these establishments, those references would offer guidance.

From a personal standpoint, I am not a huge fan of dining in formal paladares. I find that the prices are often inflated, even by western standards, and the quality of food is highly variable. In the <u>Popular and Cheap Restaurants</u> (p.159) section of this guide I review and provide directions to several sit down paladares which I found to be particularly good.

Independent Quick Food Restaurants (Street food)

A *chiringo* is a Cuban slang name given to a small, fast food dining establishment. Usually these establishments will offer only informal bench seating, or no seats at all. In almost all cases, these fast food locations operate out of the ground floor of a residential house or sometimes out of a converted carport or terrace space located at the front of the property. Some are nothing more than food carts, cooking and selling items on a street corner. Regardless of where they may be situated, most of the food sold at these locations is homemade daily.

While very popular with locals, foreigners are often reluctant to try food from these street side vendors. There is a perception that these locations are unhygienic or that they offer inferior quality food. In reality, the truth is the exact opposite. These small restaurateurs pay high taxes to operate their businesses and the Cuban health authorities routinely inspect the locations. From my experience, most of the food sold from these locations is both unique and of very high quality. From simple, glazed donuts, to the most elaborate pork and rice dishes, served in cardboard takeaway boxes called *cajitas*, these chiringos offer a very low cost, quick, and delicious way to experience Cuban cuisine.

Menus often change throughout the day and most selections are priced at 10 pesos (MN) or less. Trust the locals to know which chiringos offer the best foods at the cheapest prices. These locations will often have long lineups, stretching out onto the sidewalk, and it is common for the best operators to sell out of food after particularly busy periods. When I see a large crowd of locals around a particular chiringo, I always join the line and eagerly await tasting whatever specialty they are serving.

State-Run Cafeterias and Fast Food Locations

Due to deregulation in the restaurant industry, the prevalence of state-run cafeterias has diminished. Many can still be found around locations where there is a large population of government workers, such as near popular transit lines, hospitals and universities. These locations offer a similar mix of foods as most private chiringo locations, such as sandwiches, fried meats, eggs, hamburgers and hotdogs, but at an even lower cost. Hamburgers and most sandwiches are priced at about 5 to 10 pesos (MN). Egg sandwiches usually cost no more than 3 pesos (MN). These locations also sell a wide variety of alcohols, juices, tobacco products, candies and condoms.

There are also a fair number of state-run, fast food chains. Most of these locations offer typical, American-style fast food items. Prices are generally low and service is rapid. The main appeal of these fast food restaurants is that they are usually open 24 hours per day. They have names such as El Rapido (selling hamburgers and French fries), La Casa del Perro Caliente (jumbo hot dogs) or Dino's Pizza (pizza).

Interesting Fact: Regardless of the type of restaurant, tipping is never obligatory or expected. This goes for any service in Cuba, whether it be for housekeeping at a hotel or a ride in a taxi. That being said, it is still common for foreigners to leave small tips when they receive good service. Leaving a 5% gratuity on a 10 CUC meal bill would be considered average. Handing the hotel bellhop a quarter for delivering your suitcase to your room is always well received.

Cuban Cuisine

Resort Meals

The quality of food is probably one of the biggest complaints I hear from tourists who travel to Cuba and stay at all inclusive resorts. Although the complaints are sometimes valid, fundamentally, the problems stem from tourist expectations and Cuban marketing.

On a resort, the buffets will offer an assortment of traditional Cuban dishes as well as some international meal choices. À la carte restaurants on the resorts will also offer cuisine-specific meals, such as French specialties, Italian pasta dishes or Asian inspired meals. 24-hour snack bars will offer hot dogs, hamburgers and French fries.

The traditional Cuban dishes will usually be made to a very high standard. The meals often consist of either pork or chicken, along with sides of rice and beans, and a cucumber salad. While, to many foreigners, this might sound like a rustic meal, unworthy of presentation in a 4 star resort, this is, in fact, the quintessential Cuban meal, served to locals and visiting dignitaries alike. Foreigners who try these dishes are usually pleasantly surprised by their authenticity and rich flavor.

The complaints usually arise from the non-traditional Cuban food options which are offered at resort restaurants. The Italian pizzas and pasta plates are bland. Asian inspired dishes such as noodles or sushi will never match expectations. The standard American staples such as hamburgers and French fries will often be good, but not taste exactly like burgers from McDonald's or Burger King.

Most resorts will offer sections in their buffets where chefs will cook you a custom meal as you wait. This can range from making a custom ordered pizza or pasta dish, to grilling a pork chop or frying a seafood platter. These custom meal locations will be the gastronomic highlight of the buffets and the food is usually well worth the wait. Since all the food is prepared and cooked fresh, as you watch, you know that the ingredients are of high quality and the chef can prepare your plate perfectly to your liking. If you have special food needs, get to know your server. Sit in the same area for each meal and greet your server when you arrive. The waiters aim to please. They might not be able to honor your request on your first day but they will make an effort to get you what you need for the remainder of your stay. (for example, fresh juice outside of breakfast, unsweetened yogurt, different vegetarian options)

Traditional Cuban Meals

Outside of a resort setting you can expect to encounter a lot more traditional Cuban food choices. Below are some examples of the most common types of foods which locals cook and consume on a daily basis. The food selections are categorized by meal.

Breakfast

Breakfast is usually a small and quick meal in Cuba. The most common breakfast foods are omelets (*tortillas*) served in a sandwich with some cheese (*queso*) and/or ham (*jamon*). Bread (*pan*) with a generous dollop of butter (*mantequilla*) or a bowl of fresh fruit is another common option.

A daily ritual for many Cubans involves buying a quick breakfast from a local fast food stand on their way to work. A fresh omelet sandwich can usually be had for about 3 to 5 pesos (MN). Cups of fresh squeezed juice (*jugo natural*) usually cost only 2 pesos (MN). For those looking for a quick dose of sugar, homemade, honey-glazed donuts are sold on almost every street corner. Shots of espresso coffee usually cost only 1 peso (MN).

Lunch

As the nation's economy improves, and as more independent food stands pop up, it is becoming popular for Cubans, especially those with higher paying jobs, to purchase lunches from local fast food restaurants. The most popular lunchtime foods are sandwiches, as they are relatively inexpensive and quick to eat. Cuban sandwiches usually consist of a fat loaf of crusty bread filled with sliced ham, cucumber, and cheese. A tomato or some ketchup sauce is also usually added.

Dinner and Full Meals

In Cuba, the evening meal is the most important. It is a time when a large meal is prepared and the whole family gathers around the dinner table to eat and talk. This is a tradition that is still very active in Cuba.

The most common traditional Cuban dinner meals involve pork or chicken, served with beans and rice. Most Cuban homes do not have an oven, only a small stove-top and perhaps a slow cooker, so the meat portions are usually fried or stewed. Pork is either breaded and fried (*escalope*) or fried plain (*bistec*). The chicken may also be battered and fried or fried plain. A lemon-garlic sauce called *mojo* is sometimes drizzled over the meat or used as a marinade, to add extra flavor. The meat portions are usually small. The majority of the meal is composed of beans (*frijoles*) and rice (*arroz*). When red beans and rice are cooked together, the dish is called *congri*. If black beans and rice are cooked together, the mix is called *arroz moro*. On occasion, the beans and rice will be cooked separately and then mixed together at the table. This dish is simply called *arroz con frijoles.*
A dish called *ropa vieja* is one of the most popular traditional dishes on the island. It consists of a bed of rice and beans topped with a generous portion of stewed, pulled pork.

Another pork dish which you are likely to see a lot is called *fricase de cerdo*. This is a stewed pork dish, where the chunks of meat are extremely tender and served in a light, tomato sauce.

Soups and stews are very popular as well, namely because they are very easy to prepare. The most traditional stew is called *caldosa*. It's made from a variety of vegetables mixed together in a large pot and slow cooked. Different meats are also usually added for flavor. Despite its rustic nature, it's a delicious and healthy stew, particularly popular on cooler evenings, as it is an excellent way to warm up. Other popular soups are *crema de queso* and *crema de Virginia*. These are rich soups made of melted cheese. They make the perfect, gluttonous evening meal after a hard days work. I recommend trying a soup with every meal.

Popular Side Dishes:

- Cucumber salad, consisting of thinly sliced cucumbers drizzled with light oil and vinegar and a sprinkling of salt.
- Avocados with salt and vinegar
- Fried plantain chips (*tostones*)
- Fried pork fat or skin (*chicharones*)

Another popular component of most meals is a food group which Cubans refer to as *vianda*. In simplest terms, *vianda* is a word used to describe root vegetables and tubers which are high in carbohydrates. These include potatoes, sweet potatoes, yuca, calabaza, malanga, and plantains. A portion of *vianda* will be included in most meals, especially at restaurants. The *vianda* items will either be boiled, grilled, steamed or fried.

Desserts

Popular desserts include flan, shortbread cookies (*tortica*), pudding (*natilla*), Jello (*gelatina*), ice cream (*helado*) or donuts (*rosquillas*). Fruits are also popular dessert options.

Special Occasions

Some meals are a little more time consuming to prepare, and their ingredients are a bit more costly. Despite being part of the Cuban tradition, they are generally prepared only on special occasions. One such dish is called *cerdo asado* (roasted pork). The pork, either whole or just the leg, is marinated overnight in a lemon/garlic *mojo* sauce and then roasted for hours either in an oven or over an outdoor barbeque pit. The resulting meat is moist and filled with flavor while the pork skin is salty and crunchy.

You will also be able to find this dish at most restaurants in Cuba, although the quality varies considerably. In a restaurant, the price for a plate of roasted pork is usually very cheap, and should never cost more than 5 CUC. When hosting large parties or family events, it is becoming increasingly popular for Cubans to order a whole leg of roasted pork, cooked and delivered directly to their door. The legs will usually cost about 50 to 70 CUC but they still provide a great value, considering that one can feed approximately 30 people.

<u>Interesting Fact:</u> Even when the average Cuban goes to a restaurant to eat, simple Cuban cuisine is still the most popular item on the menu. This is not only because it is usually the cheapest item, but also because most Cubans have become very accustomed to eating the same meals on a daily basis. Some people, especially those from the older generation, would not consider a meal complete without a generous serving of rice and beans, or a small fillet of fried pork. Most restaurants cater to this preference by always including inexpensive traditional Cuban dishes on their menus, under the title of *ofertas* which means specials. These specials are always considerably less expensive than other menu options and include portions of pork or chicken, as well as rice, beans and a small salad.

Notes On Specific Cuban Foods

Breads

Cuba is known for its breads and pastries. Thousands of state-run bakeries can be found in all the cities and towns and it is a daily ritual for Cubans to line up in the morning to get their bread rations and to stock up on other baked goods. The bakeries are known as *panaderias*. Each Cuban is entitled to one mini loaf of bread (*un pan*) per day at the very nominal price of only 5 cents (MN) each. This price equates to a fraction of a penny. Additional breads cost 1 peso (MN) each. The breads are available in either soft (*suave*) or crusty (*duro*) form. Foreigners are also permitted to buy as many breads as they want, at the standard price of 1 peso (MN) each.

Most panaderias also offer other types of bread in a multitude of different sizes and shapes, as well as fresh pastries such as shortbread cookies (*torticas*), mini cakes (*marquesitas*) and glazed sweet breads.

Beef

The prevalence of pork and chicken in Cuban cuisine is due mostly to the fact that it is illegal to butcher cows in Cuba. This is not for any religious reason, but rather because the dairy situation on the island is always precarious and the government insists on using the few cows which the island does have exclusively for milk production. While beef can sometimes be found as a specialty menu item at certain state-run restaurants, for the most part it is rare or non existent.

Most of the beef which is available is imported. This usually means that it is both expensive and not fresh. Beef hamburger patties can be found in upscale restaurants and tourist resorts, but these patties are almost always of the frozen variety. The great majority of fresh hamburgers which you will encounter are made with either pork or lamb meat.

As the economy has started to improve, some large supermarkets have started to carry a small selection of imported beef products. Due to their price, they are considered a delicacy among local Cubans.

Interesting Fact: Killing a cow in Cuba is a criminal offense and a relatively bad one, too. Even if the cause of death is accidental or of natural causes, it is the Ministry of the Interior's job to conduct a full investigation. Some Cubans joke that it is a greater criminal offense to kill a cow than it is to kill another Cuban.

Fruits and vegetables

Some of the most popular fruits in Cuba are pineapples (*piña*), bananas (*platano*), oranges (*naranja*), papaya (*fruta bomba*) and mangos. You are probably already familiar with these fruits. But in your exploration of Cuba you are also likely to encounter exotic fruits which you might not recognize, such as *guayaba*, *mamey* and *chirimoya*.

Guayabas are small fruits, about the size of a peach, which grow on trees throughout the Cuban countryside. Many locals also plant guayaba trees in their back yards. The fruit's skin turns to a dark red color when perfectly ripe. Guayabas are commonly pressed into juice *(jugo de guayaba)* and this pulpy, purple nectar is served throughout the country. Guayabas are also processed into a thick, sweet paste, usually sold in blocks at local markets and state stores. This *dulce de guayaba* is similar to marmalade, and is often used as a breakfast food. It can be spread on bread *(pan con guayaba)* or used as a filling for various types of cakes and pastries.

Mamey is the national fruit of Cuba. While *mamey* is grown throughout Central America, it is very uncommon in other parts of the world. *Mamays* have a tough brown skin and are about the same size and shape as small apples. When ripe, they are sweet but usually still quite tough. They are commonly blended to make juice or milkshakes.

Chirimoyas are soft fruits, about the size of grapefruits, with smooth green skin. When perfectly ripe they taste like a mix between pineapple and banana. In Cuba they are commonly pressed into juice but some locals also enjoy chilling them briefly and then using a spoon to scoop out their creamy, white interior.

In terms of vegetables, Cubans tend to use a lot of tomatoes, cucumbers, onions, garlic and green peppers in their cooking. Salads usually consist of sliced cucumbers and tomatoes topped with a few slices of onion, and drizzled with oil and vinegar.

Popular Cuban Drinks

Coffee

Coffee can probably be considered the most popular Cuban drink. Coffee beans are also among the three most popular items exported out of the country by foreign travelers (the others being alcohol and tobacco products). Espresso-style coffee is the standard. Some tourist resorts offer American-style coffee as well, but this is rare. On resorts, cappuccinos, cafe con leche and other coffee inspired drinks are very popular.

Most Cuban households brew their coffee in old fashioned, aluminum *cafeteras*. Many state-run cafeterias and independently-run paladares and chiringos also use this method. Only large bars and fancy tourist restaurants and resorts have professional espresso machines.

Fresh roasted coffee beans can be purchased at most supermarkets and small stores. *Cubanita* is one of the most popular brands, but there are several others. A wide selection of roasted coffee is also available at airport stores. There are very few places for foreigners to find coffee beans at bargain prices in Cuba. Generally, roasted bean prices are on par with European and American coffee bean rates and are mostly uniform throughout the island. It is always more cost effective to buy a cup of coffee rather than to brew your own.

Juices

Given the abundance of fresh fruit in Cuba, it is no wonder that fruit juice is hugely popular. All restaurants and fast food joints will offer a selection of natural juices (*jugos naturales*) and the price will usually be about 2 to 3 pesos (MN) per cup. Pineapple, *guayaba*, mango, and orange are the most popular juice choices. For more exotic flavors, you can sometimes find juice made from tamarind (*tamarindo*), papaya (*fruta bomba*), *mamey* or *chirimoya*.

The juices are usually of very high quality, most being freshly pressed on the premises where they are sold. Markets also sell fresh juice in larger portions. Typically a 1 liter bottle of juice can be purchased for about 20 pesos (MN).

In most cases, when you purchase a serving of juice at a street-side restaurant, it will come served in a glass cup. After you drink it, you must return the cup to the store counter, where it is promptly washed and reused. You are also free to bring your own reusable cup or bottle, which the server will gladly fill.

Guarapo Frio

Another extremely popular juice choice is *guarapo frio*. This is freshly pressed sugar cane juice, served with crushed ice. *Guarapo frio* is sweet, nutritious, refreshing and cheap. It is only sold at specialized, state-run *guarapera* stands which are scattered throughout all towns and cities. It normally sells for only 1 peso (MN) per cup.

In many ways, the *guarapo frio* stands also act like meeting points for friends and locals. It is very common to see small crowds of people gathered at these locations, chatting about current events as they sip their cool drinks. Most Cubans also consider *guarapo* juice to have many medicinal properties, such as stimulating the immune system and improving virility. Don't let the greenish color put you off. It looks healthy and it tastes delicious. No trip to Cuba would be complete without a generous serving of *guarapo*.

Batidos

Batidos are freshly made milkshakes or fruit shakes, mixed with ice and sometimes sugar. They usually cost a bit more than simple fruit juice, but, on hot days, they provide an unmatched degree of refreshment. Popular flavors are *mamey* and *guayaba*. Some ice cream shops will also make them with fresh cream or ice cream.

Alcohol

Rum

Rum is by far the most popular alcoholic beverage in Cuba. It is cheap to buy and abundant in all state stores. It is so common, in fact, that it is even sold in small tetra-pak containers, similar to juice boxes. These single serving sizes can be purchased for less than 1 CUC. Cheaper options are available in most state stores and bodegas, where a whole bottle (700ml) can cost less than 50 pesos (MN). Cubans usually consume rum plain, but it is also the main component in almost all mixed drinks. A few of the most popular mixed drinks are listed below.

Mojito: Light rum, lime juice, fresh mint, sugar, and club soda.
Daiquiri: Rum, lime juice, sugar.
Cuba Libre: Rum and cola, with lime.
Ron Collins: Rum, lime juice and sugar, soda water.

Interesting Fact: In Cuba, the cheapest rum sometimes costs less than bottled water. There are dozens of different varieties and brands.

Beer

Beer is extremely popular in Cuba. In general, the beer in Cuba is of the pale lager variety, similar in color and taste to the average American lager. Below I have listed the major beer brands and a description of their cost and significant attributes. The beers listed below are generally referred to as the "National Brands" as they are sold in stores throughout the island.

Cristal and *Bucanero*: These are the two largest "National" beer brands. Almost all bars, discos, hotels and restaurants offer these labels. At state stores they will always cost 1 CUC. In dining or drinking establishments they will cost the same or just fractionally more. *Cristal* comes in a green can or bottle and has an alcohol content of 4.9%. *Bucanero* comes in a red and black can and has a stronger taste and an alcohol content of 5.4%.

Mayabe and *Cacique*: These beers are commonly sold in state cafeterias and restaurants which price their fares in Moneda Nacional, rather than CUC. *Mayabe* has an alcohol content of 4% and costs 18 pesos (MN). *Cacique* has an alcohol content of 4.5% and is sold for 20 pesos (MN). Since these beers are always priced in Moneda Nacional rather than in CUC, they are a very popular choice for locals and are the most common beers consumed in Cuban households.

Cheaper Beer

It is sometimes possible to find beer sold by the glass (*cerveza dispensada*) at bars in low income neighborhoods. This beer will usually only cost 5 pesos (MN) per cup, but is of a far lower quality than the national beer brands listed above. The alcohol content is low and the beer is usually rather flat.

In rural areas and lower income sectors of major cities, cheaper brands of bottled beer can be purchased for about 10 pesos (MN) per bottle. These beers are bottled by small, provincial brewers. They have a lower alcohol content and are usually a bit less carbonated than the "National Brands" listed above. These beers are never sold in supermarkets, only in cafeterias or restaurants, as the bottles are collected and returned to the manufacturers for recycling. If you are going to take the bottle out of the establishment for consumption, then you must pay an additional 3 peso (MN) charge per bottle. You are effectively paying extra to purchase the glass bottle. You do not get this money back if you later return the bottle. Popular brands include *Bruja* and *Tinima*.

Interesting Fact: In 1982 a can of beer cost 0.60 pesos (MN). That same can of beer now costs 18 pesos (MN).

Cuban Cigars

Fine cigars are one of Cuba's largest exports and one of the most popular items for tourists to take with them when they leave the island. This, coupled with the fact that some of the best Cuban cigars can be very expensive, even in Cuba, has created a huge black market for contraband and knockoff cigars.

If you look at all like a tourist, there is a 100% chance that at some point during your travels through Cuba, you will be approached by a local offering to sell you "authentic" Cuban cigars at a discount price. This happens very frequently on resorts, and the sellers are usually either Cuban hustlers (*jineteros*) walking along the beach, or members of the hotel staff at the resort. **You can be almost certain that these cigars are fake**. No matter what guarantees the seller will offer you, or how authentic the packaging, government stamps, or purchase receipts may look; the actual cigars are not genuine.

If you are not a cigar aficionado, or simply want to buy a cheap souvenir to bring back home, then these cigars might be a good deal (if you can get them cheaply enough). But if you are serious about your purchase, I would suggest that you skip the trouble and buy your cigars from legitimate state tobacco stores.

State-run tobacco shops are located on most large resorts and are scattered around popular tourist destinations and cities. The stores usually have an antique look with a large, yellow sign in front reading "La Casa del Habano." Authentic cigars are also sold in other high end state stores, many hotel souvenir shops and airport terminals. Always make sure that the cigar boxes are perfectly sealed and have government issued, holographic labels all around the edges. Always get an official purchase receipt with your order. If you are planning on leaving Cuba with more than 50 cigars, make sure to keep this purchase receipt, as you might be asked to show it at the customs checkpoint when you leave Cuba. The laws on cigar exportation will be discussed in detail in the following section.

Interesting Fact: While some of the most popular cigars sold in official tobacco shops can cost up to 20 CUC per unit, the run of the mill cigars, which are very popular with local Cubans, usually cost only 1 peso (MN) each. They are sold at almost all cafeterias and small state shops. The most popular brand name is *Reloba*. You can understand now how lucrative it can be to spend the effort to re-brand and repackage these cheap cigars, and then sell them to unknowing foreigners at a huge markup.

Bringing Back Goods

Exporting Cigars and Alcohol

Alcohol and cigars are among the most popular items for tourists to buy in Cuba to bring back with them to their countries of origin. If you plan on exporting these goods, there are some important restrictions which you should know about.

Cuban law stipulates that up to 20 loose cigars (out of a box) can be exported, per person, without having to provide any form of proof as to where the cigars were obtained. The authorities will not bother to determine if these cigars are authentic or just street level knockoffs. Furthermore, you are allowed to export a maximum of 50 cigars per person, without having to show a proof of purchase, provided that at least 30 of the cigars are contained in legitimate factory boxes with the authentic seals. It's important to note that the 50 cigar total includes the 20 loose cigars mentioned before.

In total, you are allowed to export as many cigars as you want, but for all cigars past the initial 50, you will have to provide an official proof of purchase receipt. These laws are established by Cuba in order to reduce the proliferation of cheap quality, knock off cigars and to protect the state monopoly on authentic Cuban cigars.

As for alcohol, you are allowed to export as much as you want, but you must always be certain to either pack your purchases away in your checked luggage, or to purchase your bottles of alcohol after clearing customs at the airport terminal. At most airports in Cuba, bottles of alcohol will be sold at the main terminal, and, all too often, tourists buy bottles there expecting to pass through the security checkpoints and board the plane with the bottles in their carry-on bags. This is not allowed in Cuba. As soon as the travelers reach the airplane checkpoint, these bottles of alcohol are confiscated.

If you want to take bottles of alcohol in your carry-on bags, make sure to purchase them after the security checkpoint. At every airport there will be dozens of shops and boutiques selling alcohol in the "duty free" zone after the checkpoint and before you board the plane. Also note that in most Cuban airports, when you purchase alcohol in the "duty free zone" it will usually be exactly the same price as in any other state store, but you will also be required to buy a special, clear plastic bag for your purchases, in order for them to be admissible as carry-on items. This bag costs about 1 CUC. Fundamentally, this is just a money grab and another great reason to buy your alcohol well ahead of time and pack it in your checked luggage.

Important Note: While the above section details the specifications set by the Cuban government on exports of alcohol and tobacco products, you should also check the import limitations set by the government of your own country of origin. These rules are often more stringent. As of October 2016, travelers from the United States have no monetary limit on the value of alcohol and/or tobacco products they can bring back from Cuba in their accompanied baggage.

Exporting Cuban Paintings and Art (Patrimonies)

Art is a very common thing for tourists to buy in Cuba. Usually it is in the form of paintings. They are sold throughout Cuba, not only in street fairs or bazaars, but also in private galleries and sometimes directly from an artist's home. While it is completely legal to buy art in Cuba and to take it out of the country, there are regulations.

Cuban artists who make a living selling art must be registered with the government. All articles that they sell must include a government export stamp, proving that the art is authentic and the artist is legally recognized. If you purchase art, always make certain that this stamp is included and clearly visible on the packaging. If the artist is registered with the proper authorities, then this stamp will only cost him or her a few pesos (MN) to obtain, and the price of the stamp can usually be negotiated into the total price of the artwork.

The only artists who will not want to provide you with a government export stamp are those who operate without an official license. It is still legal to buy from these vendors; however, you might be required to pay export duties on the art when you take it out of Cuba. These duties can cost anywhere from 10 to 40 CUC, or sometimes more, per piece of art.

The best way to avoid hassles is to either be absolutely sure that your art includes all the proper export stamps, or to always pack your art purchase in your checked luggage, rather than bringing it as a carry-on item, on your plane ride out of the country. If you are openly carrying a piece of art when arriving at an airport customs declaration point, you will always be directed to a special art duties area (Patrimonies Processing). Here you will have to either show the official government export stamp, or be required to pay export duties on the piece. Packing the art in your checked luggage would eliminate this hassle and expense in almost all cases.

Shopping

Shopping options in Cuba are rather limited by western standards. A network of state-operated stores (*tiendas*) and supermarkets (*supermercados*) provide household goods. Most of the locals purchase consumables and food from state-operated food depots called *bodegas*. Local markets, called *agromercados*, sell fresh produce. Street vendors sell some clothes, shoes, jewelry, art and knickknacks. Butcher shops called *carniceros*, sell meat. *Venta Libre* depots sell a similar selection of goods as *bodegas*, but at a slightly higher price and are open to both locals and foreigners.

Important Note: Remember to bring your own plastic or reusable bags when shopping. Large state supermarkets and gas stations will usually provide you with a plastic bag after your purchase, but most other small stores will not. Sometimes there will be a bag seller in the front of small stores or markets selling plastic bags (*jabas*) for 1 peso (MN) each.

Shopping Centers and Supermarkets

Shopping centers and supermarkets can be found in all cities and towns. Although locals shop at these locations, prices are usually on par or even above prices charged in North American or European stores. The items are always priced in CUC.

Shopping centers have a look that is similar to western style department stores, offering a relatively wide selection of household goods. Supermarkets are generally smaller, but still offer a good selection of processed foods, drinks, alcohol, packaged meats and frozen items. Generally, the only people who can actually afford to shop on a regular basis at these locations are affluent Cubans and foreigners. Gas stations also usually have a small convenience store located on the premises which offers a selection of packaged foods, frozen meats, alcohol and soaps. Prices and selection of goods are mostly uniform throughout all supermarkets, shopping centers and convenience stores.

Small stores, called *tiendas* or *puntos de ventas* (points of sale), offer a selection of basic consumables at identical prices to supermarkets. These shops are scattered throughout Cuban cities and towns, and the smallest ones are usually housed entirely within shipping containers placed by the side of the road. These miniature stores contain a surprisingly varied product selection and are usually staffed by two salespeople who interact with customers through a window cut out of the side of the container.

Moneda National Stores

These are stores which sell a small selection of household goods in Moneda Nacional. The stores will generally sell some soaps, construction products, and a small selection of clothes and shoes at subsidized prices. Generally these locations are dimly lit and rather hard to find. They will usually be located in poorer areas of the city. Some examples of items you can buy here are toothpaste for 7 pesos, soap for 4 pesos, and women's shoes for 12 pesos. Foreigners are welcome to shop at these stores too.

Bodegas

Cuban citizens get most of their food at small local depots called *bodegas*. These stores are everywhere throughout Cuba, with major cities having at least one located at every few street corners. Each Cuban citizen receives a tiny book, called a *libreta*, which entitles them to a monthly food ration which can be picked up from the *bodega*. This ensures that each citizen receives a healthy, minimum monthly food allowance. Cubans can also purchase supplemental quantities of food from the *bodega* at a low, state-subsidized price. Examples of goods sold at *bodegas* are staples such as rice, beans, flour, eggs and powdered milk. Some *bodegas* also sell bread.

<u>Foreigners cannot shop at bodegas</u>, only Cuban citizens with a valid *libreta* book. As a foreigner, this is the only store which you are not permitted to shop in. For every other store, if there is no "*Bodega*" sign in front, you are free to shop.

<u>Special Note:</u> The Libreta System - The tiny ration book has become a vital part of Cuba's culture since it was implemented in 1962. At first, it was a way for the Cuban government to show its commitment to the populace, by ensuring that regardless of social or economic status, each Cuban citizen would receive a base amount of food; enough to ensure a dependable nutritional intake. During the special period, the *libreta* took on even more significance, as many Cubans, faced with dire economic conditions, came to rely on the free, staple foods provided by the ration book as their largest, if not sole, source of nourishment. During the deepest parts of the special period, the average Cuban's daily caloric intake dropped to an all time low and malnutrition was a serious problem. Nevertheless, the base food provided by the *libreta* system was enough to prevent starvation.

<u>Venta Libre Depots</u>

These locations look very similar to *bodegas* and stock many of the same items. The only difference is that anybody can shop at these locations and purchase goods in whatever quantity they want. All items sold at these locations are basically sold by the state, at approximately cost price. All prices are in Moneda Nacional. Popular items are eggs, (usually sold for 1.1 pesos per unit or 40 pesos for a pack of three dozen), soaps, rum, flour and sugar. From time to time, other goods will be available such as light bulbs, hardware tools, lubricants and shoes. These depots are most commonly found in high traffic areas and especially near markets and panaderias (bakeries).

Fresh Produce Markets

From early in the morning to late in the afternoon, markets, called *agromercados* or *agropecuarios*, operate all over the island, selling produce. These markets are often crowded, noisy, and lots of fun. Vendors are usually independent farmers or sellers who work on the behalf or larger co-operative farms. Prices can vary slightly from one stall to another, depending on produce quality or ripeness, but generally the prices are uniform within each market. In richer neighborhoods, prices tend to be a bit higher than in poorer locations. Most fruits and vegetables are sold by weight, but some larger items such as pineapples usually go by unit. Prices are always in Moneda Nacional.

Carniceros

These are small butcher shop stands selling meat, deli products and sometimes cheese. By western standards, prices are cheap, with the most expensive item, *bistec de cerdo* (sliced, boneless pork loin), usually costing only 40 pesos (MN) per pound. Meat selection is usually limited to chicken or pork. Chorizo sausages are also usually available, selling for 5 pesos (MN) per link. The meat is usually fresh, and sliced right in front of you after you order, but it should be noted that refrigeration methods in these outdoor locations are lacking. It is advisable to shop for meat in the early morning, rather than in the afternoon, as you will generally get a fresher and tastier product. Remember to bring your own plastic bag or other container as these shops never provide one for free, and sometimes do not have any available for purchase.

Food Carts and Independent Produce Resellers

It is common to see little carts, laden with fruits and vegetables, being pushed around most cities and towns in Cuba. These vendors usually grow their own produce or buy it from markets and then resell it for a small mark up. They push their carts around busy streets, shouting out or singing their items and prices. Most days, around supper time, it is also common to see onion and garlic sellers walking the streets, shouting loudly to proclaim their presence. It's not a glamorous lifestyle, but these sellers provide an important service, especially of you are cooking a meal and forgot to buy a clove of garlic on your last trip to the market. Their existence adds to the charm of this island and harkens to a simple and genuine way of life.

Fairs, Street Sellers and Bazaars

In tourist areas, it is common to find outdoor street fairs selling souvenirs, jewelry, and handcrafted products. Prices are in CUC and are usually not overly expensive.

Along some busy streets, it is also common to see vendors using their front porch to sell clothes, music CDs or household items, both new and used. Prices are usually much lower than at state department stores and can be in either CUC or Moneda Nacional.

In less touristy areas, especially in poorer neighborhoods, it is common to find large indoor or outdoor flea markets and bazaars. These locations are extremely popular with locals as the prices for goods are often very low and the product selection is varied. Foreigners are welcome to shop at these locations as well. The most common items are clothes and shoes. These are usually made by local seamstresses and shoemakers (*zapateros*) or manufactured in larger Cuban factories.

Discount locations like these can be difficult to find as they are often not indicated on tourist maps. In the Shopping (p. 144) section of this guide, I include a list of bazaars and flea markets. Even if you are not looking to buy anything, they represent a great way to experience daily life and perhaps meet some interesting locals.

Cuban Lineups

It may seem like a mundane topic, but waiting in line in Cuba is a little bit different than most other places in the world. During your stay in the country, you will be doing it enough that the process warrants explanation.

Whether queuing up at a money exchange office, to order fast food, or most any other scenario, Cubans have developed an easy and clever way to ensure that order is maintained without sacrificing convenience.

In order to get into line, simply position yourself in the general area of the back of the line and call out *"El Último?"*. This means, "Who is the last person?". The last person in the line will identify themselves and you just have to stand behind them. If, later on, another person wants to get in line and calls out *"El Último?"*, you just have to identify yourself, by raising your finger or saying *"Yo!"* (me), and your position in the line has been established. Most Cubans will also ask *"Detrás de quien?"* which means, "Who are you standing behind?" This helps to ensure that even if you were to leave the line and not return, the continuum of the general queue is undisturbed. Just point to the person in front of you, the former *"Último."*

Once your position in line is established, you can feel free to leave the formal lineup. As long as you return to the line before your turn comes, your spot will be saved, as the person directly in back of you will remember that you were there before him.

For longer lineups, some particularly daring Cubans will establish their position and then go off to run errands, checking back sporadically on the progress of the line. It can sometimes be a risky move, particularly if several people in the line depart and do not return. In this scenario it can be difficult to re-establish the positioning, as there may be no witnesses to validate the claim.

The lineup in Cuba is called "*la cola*." There is a lineup for almost everything in Cuba, so even if you don't remember all the rules, you will be educated in the process rather rapidly. Most importantly, some people receive special consideration and always have a guaranteed spot at the head of the line. These include women queuing up with small children, and visibly pregnant women.

Internet In Cuba

The internet in Cuba is highly regulated. Most households which have computers can access a Cuban *intranet*, which allows them to send emails and short communications throughout Cuba and to foreign countries. For the great majority of Cubans, use of the world wide internet is not possible from a home setting. It can only be accessed from expensive internet cafes or certain workplace settings.

Public Internet WIFI Spots

In 2015 the Cuban government opened a network of public WIFI spots throughout the island. It is common to see dozens of locals and foreigners seated along the sidewalks using their phones and laptops to connect to the internet in these areas. The internet connection is not very fast, but good enough for checking emails and catching up on some news. To access the WIFI internet you must have an account set up with ETECSA (the national telecom provider) and the official cost to use the service is 2 CUC per hour of WIFI. Technically this service is only available to Cuban residents. However, beside the WIFI spots you will always find many residents reselling their access cards. 1 hour WIFI cards can usually be purchased from these resellers for about 4 CUC. If you are a foreigner, you will have to purchase your WIFI time from one of these resellers.

If you desire a more stable or robust internet connection you can use the WIFI located in higher end hotels or internet cafes throughout Cuba, which are starting to roll out these services. At all of these

84

locations, you must always pay to use the internet. Cafes and hotels generally charge about 5 to 10 CUC per hour of usage. If you did not bring a computer with you to Cuba, many hotels offer computer terminals which are connected to the internet. The cost to use the terminal and internet is sometimes slightly higher than using just the WIFI with your own device.

It is perfectly safe and legal to bring laptops and other computer devices into Cuba. It is not permitted to bring WIFI routers or other telecommunications broadcasting equipment.

A list of internet access points and prices can be found on page 151 of this guide, under the heading "Internet Access Points in Havana."

Interesting Fact: Foreign expats living in Cuba are allowed to use the internet from their home. They pay a monthly fee of about 50 CUC for this option. They are not permitted to transmit the signal via WIFI. Sharing this internet line with Cuban citizens is not permitted, but this rule is often broken without consequence.

Phones in Cuba

The Cuban national phone and internet provider is named ETECSA. This company operates throughout the island and has a virtual monopoly over all telephone and internet services. There are thousands of ETECSA offices and stores located throughout the island. They are often found in shopping centers, along busy streets, in most hotel lobbies and airports. For all your communication needs, such as getting a cell phone line, purchasing cell phone credit or purchasing phone cards, simply visit any ETECSA store.

Landlines

Most Cuban households have their own personal land line telephone. The land line telephone service is extremely cheap, with a monthly bill usually costing no more than 20 to 30 pesos (MN).

Public Phones

There is also a highly developed network of public phones in most cities and small towns. Cubans purchase calling cards which enable them to use these phones almost as cheaply as their own home phones. The calling cards are called *Tarjetas Propia*, and can be purchased in denominations of 5 or 10 pesos (MN). These cards last for hours of talk time and can be recharged in smaller or larger denominations. Foreigners are permitted to purchase these phone cards as well. They are an excellent resource to have in order to communicate with anybody on the island. The *Tarjetas Propia* cannot be used for international phone calls.

International Calling cards

The cheapest method to make international calls is to buy an international phone card (*tarjeta internacional*). These can be acquired at any ETECSA point of sale office. They cost 10 CUC. These phone cards allow you to use any land line or public phone to make international calls. The instructions on how to use the card are written on the back. You always simply dial the number 166 in order to enter the directory, and then you enter your card number and the pin. Most international calls cost between 1.40 CUC per minute (North America) and 1.50 CUC (rest of the world). While still expensive, this is the cheapest option. All other international calling cards purchased from sources outside the country will not function in Cuba. You can also use your international cards to make local calls, but this will be expensive. The best option for local calls is to use the *Tarjetas Propia,* as mentioned earlier.

Cell Phones

Despite being expensive, cell phones have become very popular over the last few years. In Cuba, all cell phone service is sold as a pay-as-you-go plan. The price for a Cuban to open a cell phone line (buy a SIM card and phone number), is 30 CUC. Thereafter, talking credit must also be purchased. A minimum of 5 CUC of talk credit must be purchased per month in order to maintain the account active. Local talk rates are 35 cents (CUC) per minute, and drop to 10 cents (CUC) at night (from 11pm to 7am). For calls between two cell phones, the caller always pays for the use. For calls between a land line and a cell phone, the cell phone user always pays. Text messages cost 9 cents (CUC) to send. All international incoming calls are free to receive. The cost to make international outgoing calls varies between 1.60 CUC per minute to North America and 1.80 CUC per minute to the rest of the world. Limited-time promotions and discounts are common, but, generally, using a cell phone for international calls is prohibitively expensive.

Only Cuban citizens are permitted to own a Cuban cell phone line. Foreigners can only rent a line. The price of this rental is 3 CUC per day, in addition to purchasing talk time credit. If you are going to be renting a cell phone line, it is best to bring your own unlocked cell phone. Note that only GSM phones (these phones are characterized by having a SIM card) which can operate on the 900mhz spectrum will work in Cuba. Most modern cell phones meet this requirement. Talk rates are the same as mentioned in the above paragraph.

<u>Foreign-based Cell Phones</u>

If you are intending on using your personal, foreign-based cell phone in Cuba, you should expect to incur expensive roaming charges. Most phone plans, even ones with international call plans, do not include Cuba. If your cell phone will be your main mode of telephone communication, make absolutely sure, before you arrive in Cuba, that your roaming plan offers competitive rates. If you do not have a suitable roaming plan, you can expect to pay about 4$ per minute on international and local calls originating in Cuba, and at least 1$ per text message.

More information about using the internet and how to use phones will be provided later in this book.

Interesting Fact: Due to the high cost of cell phone rates, Cubans have developed an innovative way to communicate. Rather than using cell phones like regular phones, most Cubans simply use them as pagers. For example, a Cuban might use their home phone to call a friend's cell phone. Instead of answering the cell phone, the friend will dismiss the call and then find a cheap public phone to call back from. This way, the cell phone is never charged because the call is never initialized.

Car Rentals

Car rentals are a popular, albeit expensive option to explore Cuba. State-run car rental outlets are located all over the island and are particularly concentrated in large cities and in tourist hot spots. Both tourists and locals can rent vehicles.

Rental rates for small cars start at about 45 CUC per day with an additional 15 CUC for insurance, which is mandatory. There is usually an additional charge of about 30 CUC for a full tank of gasoline. If you later return the vehicle with a full tank, this amount will be deducted from your total bill. Small cars are usually inexpensive, Chinese sedans and compacts. They are adequate, but offer very few frills. Larger cars and luxury vehicles are also available, but daily rental rates are much higher.

When renting a car in Cuba it is important to watch for scams. Make sure that you receive an official, computer printed receipt for all the services you are paying for. If possible, try to pay for the transaction with your credit card. All credit card transactions are processed through corporate channels, so fraudulent transactions are uncommon. The vast majority of scams are perpetuated when clients pay for rental services in cash. Furthermore, always inspect the vehicle before taking possession and, if possible, snap a few photos of the outside, especially if there are scratches or damaged areas on the vehicle. Always return the vehicle with a full tank of gas.

VERY IMPORTANT: It cannot be stressed enough - Be extremely careful when driving in Cuba! If you get into an accident in Cuba, even a minor one, you will be forced to remain on the island until an accident investigation is completed. This can sometimes take months. This is one of the main reasons foreigners are discouraged from renting vehicles in Cuba. There are dozens of stories of tourists who rented cars, had minor accidents and were then forced to stay in Cuba while a police or court-ordered investigation was conducted. This process is part of Cuban law and it cannot be modified or changed, even with the intervention of foreign embassies.

Furthermore, it should be noted that if you are involved in a serious traffic accident in Cuba, which results in bodily injury or death, there is a good chance that you will face some jail time. The concept of a "no fault" vehicle crash is not practiced in Cuba, and the excuse of a collision being "accidental" will not be accepted. Drive at your own risk.

Health Insurance and the Cuban Medical System

As a tenet of the revolution, all Cuban citizens receive 100% free medical care throughout the island. The Cuban health care system has a reputation for being very good. Most major cities have large, modern hospitals as well as hundreds of local clinics.

As a foreigner, you will have to pay for most medical procedures. Prices vary widely depending on which medical problem you have and which hospital you visit. While minor problems will be inexpensive, the bills can add up rapidly for more serious ailments. For this reason, it is always highly recommended to have full medical travel insurance when visiting Cuba. Medical travel insurance is usually available relatively inexpensively from online-based insurance brokers, and the cost to have the insurance with zero deductible is usually only nominally more. I always recommend this option. This will assure you that whatever might happen in Cuba, you can always visit the best hospital and receive world class service, and your insurance will cover the whole bill.

If you do not have insurance and your medical issue is minor, you can usually get by with simply visiting a local hospital or clinic and paying the doctor on duty a small sum of money. 5 to 10 CUC will be more than enough to cover a simple consultation and perhaps some bandaging for cuts and scrapes. If your condition is more serious and you have to be admitted to the hospital, you will officially have to be registered into the Cuban medical system, and the fees will be higher.

Smaller hospitals in Cuba generally look a bit dated and can sometimes be crowded. Larger, modern hospitals look very similar to western facilities. In areas with a high concentration of foreigners, there will usually be a few large hospitals which specifically cater to non-Cubans. While these facilities offer the most state of the art services, they will also be the most expensive. If you have insurance, then definitely go to one of these locations for treatment. If you lack insurance and are afraid of running up high medical bills, a smaller hospital will usually be most cost effective, and the service will be similar.

Do You Need Medical Insurance?

While all foreigners visiting Cuba are legally required to have medical insurance coverage, customs officials almost never verify this information. So, while technically, insurance is required, in practice, most tourists do not have any when they visit Cuba. In any case, if a situation occurs where you want, or need, to purchase insurance after you land in Cuba, you can always do so, at a relatively cheap cost. Insurance offices located in the arrivals terminals at most Cuban airports will sell medical insurance for about 3 CUC per day.

Special Note: If you go to a smaller hospital and anticipate paying in cash for your treatment, always withhold your payment until you have received treatment and then, only pay the actual doctor, and not other members of the hospital staff. Doctors and trained medical personnel are usually very professional, but the same cannot always be said for the orderlies, technicians and reception staff. If anybody asks you for an upfront payment just to see the doctor, it is likely that they are trying to scam you. You should immediately demand to speak to the hospital administrator.

Giving Donations and Gifts

It is common for foreigners to bring small gifts to give out to local Cubans. While gifts and donations are never expected, they are always well received. Considering that the average Cuban is relatively poor and the cost of goods in the country is relatively high, most Cubans do not have much economic slack to spend on non-essentials. Furthermore, due to the American embargo, it is often expensive or impossible to purchase certain foreign goods. Small, everyday items, which foreigners take for granted, are considered major gifts in Cuba and will make a huge difference to the recipient. Handing out small gifts will also make you instantly popular with locals and is a great way to make friends. These friends will open hundreds of doors for you and help you to understand the country and culture. Don't feel shy at all about giving gifts. The average Cuban is proud, but they are more than happy to accept friendly donations.

It is important to note that if you are planning to bring some gifts, you do not have to go out of your way to purchase new items. You can save a lot of money by simply bringing used items, which are still in working condition. Perhaps you have a few old, but functional, things around your house that you were planning to throw out, or sell at a garage sale. Consider bringing them to Cuba instead.

The best gifts are small household items and clothes. Towels make great gifts since in Cuba they can be expensive and are often of poor quality. The same goes for bed sheets. Shoes are also key items. It is not uncommon for Cubans to wear their shoes well after most westerners would say they had reached expiration. Cubans repair their shoes constantly and try to make them last as long as possible. A good, comfortable pair of walking shoes will be a life changer. If you feel uncomfortable giving away old shoes, you can simply leave the shoes on the side of the road. In no time, somebody will pass by to claim them as their own. Kid's shoes are especially prized.

Clothing and accessories such as t-shirts, caps, underwear, socks, jeans and backpacks are always great. Baby clothing is also much appreciated. Just keep in mind that the climate in Cuba is hot, so don't plan on giving away winter outerwear.

Books are another fantastic gift option. While Spanish books are abundant on the island, foreign language books are very rare. A few English, French or German books or magazines will make a huge difference to somebody trying to learn a foreign language. Along this same theme, electronic media such as recent movies and popular television shows are always in strong demand, especially by teens. A few DVDs or a small USB memory stick filled with media would represent a very thoughtful gift.

Note: Most Cubans have a computer in their home (usually a very basic one) or can use one at work or school.

Guitar strings are expensive to buy in Cuba and are perpetually in short supply. A set of new strings would make a meaningful impact on a Cuban musician's life.

Miscellaneous other items include work gloves, feminine hygiene products, diapers, hair elastics, sunscreen, deodorant, antiperspirants, diaper rash cream, infant teething toys and cutlery such as knives and forks.

If you happen to have an old cell phone lying around your house, you might consider bringing it to donate to a Cuban. Cell phones are very expensive in Cuba, and even one that is obsolete by western standards will see many more years of use in Cuba. Note that only GSM phones (these phones are characterized by having a SIM card), which can operate on the 900mhz spectrum, will work in Cuba. Unlocked cell phones are best, but cell phones can be unblocked in Cuba at a relatively low cost.

Money is also a great gift under the right circumstances. Even just a small monetary gift of $10 would represent a week's salary for a Cuban, so it will certainly be well received.

Donating Toys

At first glance you might think that bringing toys as a donation might not have a lot of merit. In fact, they are among some of the most desperately wanted items in Cuba. The average Cuban child might possess only a single toy, if he or she is lucky. Most have none at all. It is common to see dozens of children in a park on the weekend, all sharing just one broken soccer ball, or little girls waiting in line to play with a doll. Foreigners often dismiss toys as donation items because they are viewed as non-essential. They are also extremely expensive to purchase on the island (a simple doll might cost 15 CUC) so most Cuban parents cannot afford them. For these reasons, toys are almost non-existent in Cuba. I highly recommend them as donations, as they will make both children and parents very happy, and you know they will be used and cherished for a long time. And since Cuban children are so good at sharing, your donation will bring joy to a whole neighborhood of kids.

Most desired toys:

- Tennis balls and baseballs (or any other type of ball)
- Dolls
- Action figures
- Miniature cars
- Coloring books
- Stickers
- Art supplies

It is not advised to give computerized devices, such as video games, or toys which require batteries. These items will not likely be of much use as batteries are rather expensive.

How To Give A Gift

Some guides suggest handing all donations directly to government offices or to foreign aid organizations so that they can be distributed throughout the island to those most in need. This route is extremely bureaucratic and there is no assurance that the items will actually reach the intended recipients.

The best strategy is to go to a park in a poor neighborhood and just hand out items to kids and parents. Even if the items are not used directly by the recipients, they will be shared with other family members or sold to other Cubans at a low cost. If you are staying at a casa particular, you can also give gifts directly to the casa landlord. Either way, you will be directly and immediately helping the locals, while making friends in the community.

Donating Medicine

You are free to bring up to 10 kilograms of medicine into Cuba, duty free. This is an option that some visitors choose. There are many foreign aid organizations which will freely provide packages of medicine and medical supplies for you to import into Cuba, with specific instructions on how and where to donate the goods. This is completely legal and is considered humanitarian aid. While this may be a good option for some visitors, the need for additional medicine in Cuba is not as pressing as some might suggest. While the Cuban government does not have large stockpiles of drugs like most western countries, their medical system is relatively well developed and there are enough medications and supplies for the people who need them. An additional suitcase full of gauze and Advil wouldn't hurt, but it will not be meeting a desperate need. More information about donating medicine can be found online or at the following website: www.njt-pqt.org

<u>Special Note:</u> Although all donations are welcome, you should be aware that donations of soap, shampoo, toothpaste and toilet paper are among the most common. Most locals, especially those working with tourists, have more than enough of these items. Furthermore, Cubans can purchase them very inexpensively themselves.

Leaving Cuba

Since May 1, 2015, there is no longer an airport departure tax to leave Cuba. In the past, all foreigners had to pay a 25 CUC exit tax to leave the country. This fee has been completely abolished.

Certain outdated websites and tourist guides still mention this airport tax. Rest assured that it is no longer applicable and there are no plans to bring it back. There is no fee to leave the country.

General Havana Information

Getting to Havana Cheaply

<u>Direct Flights</u>

The easiest way to get to Havana is via a direct flight. The Havana airport (José Martí International Airport) is located about 20 kms south of the city and receives most international flights at Terminal 3 (USA flights usually use Terminal 2). The airport is relatively modern and has been undergoing extensive renovations for some time, as the Cuban government prepares to grow its tourism economy.

Once you exit the airport, you must take a taxi to get to the city of Havana. Unless you have a friend in Havana who can personally pick you up, or you are traveling as part of a planned tour group with a tour bus included, taking an airport taxi is your only choice to get to the city. There is no public transportation between the airport and Havana.

Hailing a taxi at the airport is very straightforward. In fact, there is usually a large crowd of taxi drivers waiting at the arrivals gate, all very eager to offer you a ride to town. A taxi transfer usually costs about 25 to 30 CUC. It is expensive, and you are very unlikely to be able to negotiate this price. As with many airports around the world, the taxi drivers have banded together to maintain strict pricing.

If you will be staying at a casa particular in Havana, you should give the taxi driver the address of the casa immediately upon entering the vehicle. Make certain that the driver takes you to the address that you specified. It is a common scam in Cuba for taxi drivers to take unsuspecting foreigners to different casas, sometimes ever to their own homes, in order to make extra commissions. Sometimes drivers will try to dissuade you from going to your pre-booked casa, saying that it is not a good place, or perhaps that it is no longer available.

This is almost always a scam. The best approach is to simply insist that the driver takes you to the exact address that you have, and then to verify for yourself, once you reach the destination, that the address is correct.

If you are staying at a casa particular in Havana, most landlords will insist that they pick you up from the airport themselves (if they have a vehicle) or that they send a taxi driver to the airport to pick you up directly. These drivers will usually be waiting outside the arrivals gate with a sign that says your name. The price for this service is usually the same as a standard airport transfer, and sometimes might be a bit cheaper. The main advantage is that you will avoid the taxi scams and arrive to your prearranged accommodations without delay or hassle. If you want to pre-book an airport taxi transfer for your next trip, you can do so at the following website: www.BestCubaGuide.com/Taxis. The cost is 25 CUC, payable directly to the taxi driver, upon arrival.

Note: It is always advised to exchange a bit of money at the CADECA exchange office located inside the airport, upon arrival. The airport exchange offices are open 24 hours per day, and rates are comparable to exchange offices in the city. Even if you simply exchange 100 CUC, this will easily give you enough money to pay for your airport transfer and your first night in Havana. Exchanging some money at the airport is crucial if you are arriving on a late flight since most exchange offices in the city of Havana will close at about 7pm or earlier.

Fly to Varadero

Despite being the capital city of Cuba, there are not that many airlines which offer frequent, direct flights to Havana. Furthermore, most of the airlines which service Havana do not offer any discount flight options. If you are able to get a suitable direct flight to Havana, at an agreeable price, you should definitely reserve it. But, if the prices just seem too high, do not lose hope; there is another option.

As mentioned before, Varadero is a massive resort town located just 2 hours away from Havana. Varadero has an international airport which is serviced by hundreds of airlines. International flights to Varadero are not only much more common than those going to Havana, but they are usually considerably cheaper, too. Sometimes the savings can amount to 50%. If you want to visit Havana but are looking for the most budget friendly options, you should definitely consider booking a cheap flight to Varadero. The Varadero airport is located just 130 km away from downtown Havana, and there are many cheap options to get you from the Varadero airport directly to Havana.

<u>Varadero Airport to Havana by Bus</u>

If you are landing at the Varadero airport and planning to go directly to Havana, you can take the Viazul bus <u>directly from the airport</u>. The Viazul bus going from Varadero to Havana departs 3 to 4 times per day and travels from the town of Varadero all the way to Havana. On every trip, the bus stops to pick up and drop off passengers at the Varadero airport. The bus stops directly in front of the departures area of the airport. Once you land in Varadero and get out of the airport terminal, simply turn left and walk about 10 meters. You will be standing in front of the Departures terminal. The Viazul bus will arrive at this location according to the schedule indicated below.

<u>Note:</u> There is no terminal and there is no Viazul signage. But simply stay in this location, and rest assured that the bus will come. There are usually other foreigners waiting in this area too, all for the Viazul bus.

The Viazul bus is white, with a large Viazul logo printed on the side. It is difficult to miss. When the bus comes, simply ask the driver if you can buy a ticket to ride to Havana. The fare is 10 CUC. Space is limited, but usually sufficient. The bus usually does not wait around very long, so be sure to have all your baggage in order and your money in hand.

Varadero Airport to Havana Bus Schedule

From	To	Departure Time	Arrival Time
Varadero Airport	Havana	12:40pm	3:15pm
Varadero Airport	Havana	4:40pm	7:15pm
Varadero Airport	Havana	8:15pm	10:55pm
--	--	--	--
Havana	Varadero Airport	6:00am	9:00am
Havana	Varadero Airport	8:00am	10:50am
Havana	Varadero Airport	1:00pm	3:35pm

This schedule changes regularly: Please verify www.Viazul.com for updated times.

Note: I do not recommend asking other bus drivers or taxi drivers for help in finding the Viazul stop or about the arrival schedule. Most of the time they will simply tell you that the bus no longer comes to the airport, or that the last bus just left and you will have to wait hours for the next one. Then they will offer to take you to Havana themselves for a *cheap* 90 CUC fare. The Cuban taxi drivers waiting at the airport are always hungry for money, and will try to take advantage of a situation to make a little extra from a confused tourist. Simply remember to wait in front of the departures door of the airport and have faith that the Viazul bus will arrive according to the schedule.

The trip from the Varadero Airport to Havana takes about 2.5 hours. Although the distance from the Varadero airport to Havana is only about 130 km, the bus makes several short stops along the way to the main Havana terminal. The bus usually makes a 5 minute stop in the city of Matanzas to pick up additional travelers. Next, the bus stops at a roadside cantina at the midway point between Varadero and Havana. This stop will usually last about 20 minutes and is a good opportunity to eat something and stretch your legs. The bus makes another quick stop in the town of Guanabo, on the outskirts of Havana.

Arriving in Havana

The Viazul bus makes 3 stops in Havana. You should get off at the stop which is closest to your destination (hotel or casa).

The first stop occurs in Downtown, Old Havana. If your hotel or housing arrangements are located in Old Havana or Central Havana, you should get off at this stop. There will be taxis waiting to bring you directly to your destination, although you will likely be within walking distance of your accommodations. Mention ahead of time to the bus driver that you want to be let off in Old Havana.

The second stop will occur about 5 minutes later, when the bus enters the Vedado neighborhood. The bus will stop near the corner of *Calle 27 de Noviembre* Street (close to 29th) and L. This location is directly beside the University of Havana and just a block away from the Habana Libre hotel. If you are staying in the Vedado neighborhood, get off at this stop. You will be within easy walking distance of all the major hotels and most of the *casas particulares* in Vedado, but you can also just take a short taxi ride to get to your destination.

Finally, the bus makes its last stop at the main Viazul bus terminal located at Calle 26 and Zoologico (26th street and the Zoo, right in front of the Havana Zoo). This is located in the Nuevo Vedado neighborhood, in the far west corner of Vedado. If you are planning to stay in Nuevo Vedado or at any of the large hotels located in the western suburbs of Havana (Miramar, Playa), then this is your stop.

Traveling from Havana to the Varadero Airport

If you need to return back to the Varadero Airport for your return flight home, it is very simple. Once again, just take the Viazul bus. The main Havana Viazul bus terminal is located at Calle 26 and Zoologico. It is recommend to purchase your ticket at least two days in advance, as this is an extremely popular route. The cost to get from Havana to the Varadero Airport is 10 CUC. The schedule is indicated above. Be aware that if you are going to the airport to catch a flight back home, you should always arrive at the airport at least 2 hours in advance of your departure.

Note: There used to be another Viazul bus terminal in Havana, located near the Plaza de la Revolución. This no longer exists. The only way to catch the Viazul bus in Havana is at the main terminal (Calle 26 and Zoologico).

The Main Viazul Terminal in Varadero

In the town of Varadero, the main Viazul bus terminal is located at the corner of Calle 36 and Autopista (the highway). Buses leave from this location to go to Havana four times per day. They also travel to most other cities in Cuba. The bus to Havana will always pass by the Varadero airport according to the times posted in the schedule above. If you are in the town of Varadero and want to take the Viazul bus from the **Varadero terminal** to Havana, the fare is 10 CUC and the route schedule is posted below. This is a very popular bus route, so make sure to buy your tickets at least a day in advance.

The bus schedule for departures and arrivals from the main Varadero Terminal in the town of Varadero to Havana is presented on the next page. Do not confuse this with the schedule presented on page 99, as that is the schedule for arrivals and departures from the Varadero Airport, which is located about 30 minutes outside the town of Varadero.

Varadero Terminal to Havana Bus Schedule

From	To	Departure Time	Arrival Time
Varadero Terminal	Havana	12:00pm (noon)	3:15pm
Varadero Terminal	Havana	4:00pm	7:15pm
Varadero Terminal	Havana	7:35pm	10:50pm
--	--	--	--
Havana	Varadero Terminal	6:00am	9:25am
Havana	Varadero Terminal	8:00am	11:15am
Havana	Varadero Terminal	1:00pm	4:00pm
Havana	Varadero Terminal	5:30pm	8:25pm

This schedule changes regularly: Please check www.Viazul.com for updated times.

Need help making travel arrangements?

Got more questions?

Real Havana is here to help!

If you require additional information or assistance in making travel arrangements, either before or during your travels in Cuba, you can post a question on the Real Havana Travel Forum, located at

www.BestCubaGuide.com/Forum

The forum is active and questions are answered very quickly.

All services promoted on www.BestCubaGuide.com are commission free and quality guaranteed.

We have negotiated exclusive, low cost deals for:

- Casas Particulares

- Long distance taxis

- Airport transfers

- Havana city tours

- Professional Havana tour guides

Plan your whole Cuba trip on our website, and get lots more info about visiting Havana!

Just check out

www.BestCubaGuide.com

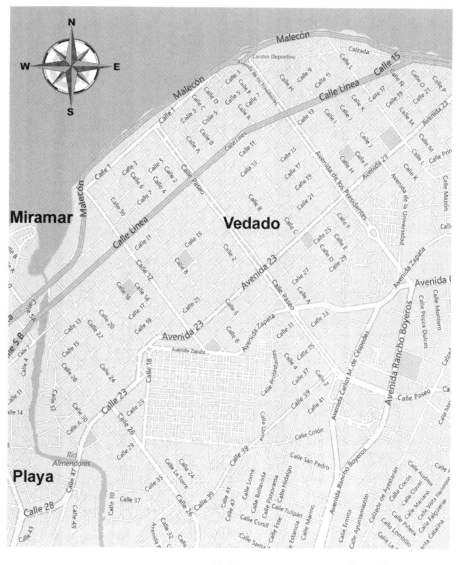

Map Of

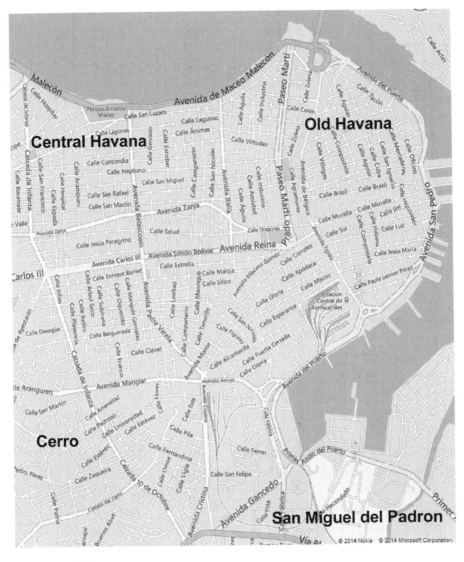

Havana

Havana's City Plan

The map on the previous page shows the city of Havana, comprising the neighborhoods of Old Havana (La Habana Vieja), Central Havana (Centro Habana) and El Vedado. Running along the northern edge of the city is a concrete sea wall. This is called the *Malecon*. It runs from the western tip of Vedado all the way to the eastern corner of Old Havana. The Bay of Havana is the large body of water located to the east of Old Havana. For a more detailed map, with all the street names clearly indicated, you should check out **www.BestCubaGuide.com/Havana-Map/**

In Old Havana and Central Havana, there is very little organization in the streets and their naming. It is easy to get momentarily lost in these neighborhoods, but the Malecon is always only a few blocks away and is a perfect landmark to help you reorient yourself.

In Vedado, the streets are mostly straight and highly organized. All of the streets are organized according to an alpha numeric system, which makes the neighborhood extremely easy to navigate. All of the roads going east and west (parallel to the Malecon) are numbered with **odd** numbers. The road running directly along the sea wall is simply called Malecon, but each successive street is named with an odd number. The word for street in Spanish is *calle*. The first street after the Malecon is named Calle 1 (1st Street). The second street is named Calle 3 (3rd Street). The third street is named Calle 5 (5th Street), and so on, going all the way to Calle 47 (47th street). At about the midway point there is Calle 23. This is the largest and busiest street in Vedado. It is also called La Rampa. It developed this name because of the long, rising slope that the street makes as it stretches west from the Malecon.

The streets going north to south (perpendicular to the Malecon) are named either with a **letter** or an **even** number. The street running through the center of Vedado is called Paseo. All parallel streets to the east of Paseo are named with a letter of the alphabet, starting with Calle A (A Street) and increasing according to the successive

106

letter of the alphabet, until Calle O (O Street). All streets west of Paseo are named with an even number, starting at (Calle 2) 2nd Street, going all the way to Calle 30.

Note that some of the locals will call certain streets by different names. Some of these names have origins before Havana's city plan was formalized. Regardless if you use the modern alpha numeric names or the older names, everybody will still understand what street you are referring to.

<u>Certain notable examples would be:</u>

Calle G, also called Avenida de los Presidentes
Calle 9, also called Linea
Calle 7, also called Calzada
Malecon, also called Washington
Salvador Allende, also called Carlos Tercero, (later becomes Simón Bolívar and finally Reina Street)
Ave del Puerto in old Havana is also called Maceo or San Pedro
Prado, in front of the Capitolio building is also called Paseo de Marti
Ave. de Italia is also called Galiano
Brasil is also called Teniente Rey
Manglar is also called Arroyo
Máximo Gómez is also called Monte

Addresses

Addresses are typically written down as being located between one street and another. The Spanish word for between is *entre*, and it is usually abbreviated as e/. So, the address of a building located on G Street, between 23 and 25, would be written as Calle G e/ 23 y 25. If a building is at the corner, then the Spanish word *esquina* is used (abbreviated as *esq.*). A location at the corner of 23 and M would be written as Calle 23, esq. M. Sometimes the words *bajos* and *altos* are also used in addresses to indicate the level of a particular apartment. If the apartment is located on the ground floor, it would be referred to as a *bajos* (low) unit. A top floor apartment is called an *altos* (high) unit.

Neighborhoods and Places of Interest

Havana is the capital of Cuba and the largest city on the island. It can be hot and humid; dirty and broken. It is a mix of old and new; ugly and beautiful. It is a perfect canvas to showcase a fascinating and unpretentious culture, in a vibrant, historic atmosphere.

The main city is broken up into 3 neighborhoods (*barrios*), each with their own architecture and personality: Old Havana, Central Havana and Vedado.

Old Havana

Of the three main neighborhoods of Havana, Old Havana is the smallest. It is also the one where most of the tourists go. In a way, it is a well preserved tourist attraction. Old Havana was once Havana's port district, and is the site of the earliest settlements in the city. The streets are tight and, for the most part, paved in cobblestones. During the day there are thousands of people walking along the main roads. There are museums and boutiques and restaurants. It is clean and there are police on almost every street corner. It is absolutely safe, day and night.

Many of the streets in Old Havana are closed to car traffic, thus making it a pedestrian sanctuary. Most of the people walking in Old Havana are tourists. Along the street you will find hundreds of tiny, family-operated, fast food stands selling pizza, sandwiches, and ice cream.

There are many squares and restaurant terraces where you can sit in and around Old Havana. The maze of streets makes it a perfect place for you to spend a day browsing and enjoying the city. Old Havana is not large, so it is almost impossible to get completely lost. The Bay Of Havana encircles Old Havana on three sides, so you should always be able to orient yourself. If all else fails, simply ask where *El Capitolio* (the Capitol building) is located. It's on the border of Old Havana and Central Havana, so that will always give you a great reference point.

Since Old Havana is a major tourist spot, you can also expect to find many local Cubans hanging around the area, trying to glean a bit of money from the relatively rich foreigners. There are a lot of *jineteros* in this neighborhood. As you stroll around the most popular sights, people on the street will, undoubtedly, ask you for money. It is not advisable to give them any. Many locals will try to strike up friendly conversations in order to gain your trust. Later they will either ask you directly for money, or try to sell you products or services. You should probably assume that if a local in Old Havana is being very nice to you and offering to show you some special attractions or to take you to a special restaurant, then he or she is soon going to request a bit of money, as well. They might only ask for a few dollars, but as soon as you give it to them, they will likely ask for more, and it will be hard to get rid of them. It is best just to be polite and say no from the beginning.

Places of Interest

<u>El Capitolio (The Capitol Building)</u>

El Capitolio is a large domed building, located on Prado Street, on the border of Old Havana and Central Havana. It was modeled after the American Capitol building in Washington D.C. The large manicured campus directly beside the Capitol building is called the Parque Central. Just north of the Capitolio you will notice the **Gran Teatro de La Habana,** which is one of the most ornately designed buildings in Havana and where the national ballet performs. The Capitolio is an important landmark for orienting yourself in the city. The building faces east and everything in front of it is Old Havana. The neighborhood of Central Havana starts west of the building (behind it).

<u>Prado Street (Paseo de Marti)</u>

Prado is the street directly in front of the Capitolio. It designates the border between Old Havana and Central Havana. It runs from the Malecon all the way to the Capitolio, before it curves slightly west and changes name to become Calle Maximo Gomez. It continues to designate the border of the two neighborhoods for a considerable distance further.

More importantly, Prado, particularly the area around the Capitolio, acts as a central traffic hub for the city. Communal taxis coming into the city, or driving to the outskirts, almost always stop on Prado, in front of the Capitolio building, and it often acts as either the beginning or end of their route.

<u>Obispo Street</u>

Obispo is the largest shopping street in Old Havana. It is highly tourist-oriented and lined with upscale boutiques selling art, crafts, souvenirs and clothing. On a weekend this street will be so crowded that you will have trouble walking. The crowds and commerce spill out onto side streets as well.

Plaza Vieja (Intersection of Muralla and San Ignacio)

There are dozens of public squares in Old Havana but the **Plaza Vieja** is the most popular. It's ringed by dozens of restaurants and cafes. Although it can get very hot during the afternoons, in the morning it makes for a great location to have a relaxing coffee as you people watch and enjoy the old architecture of the surrounding buildings.

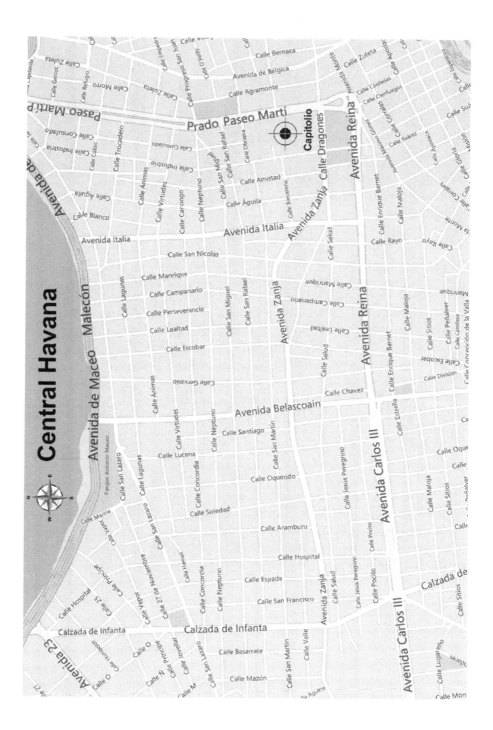

Central Havana

Central Havana is located just west of Old Havana. Central Havana is a bustling, noisy, dirty and authentic Cuban experience. In contrast to Old Havana, in Central, most of the people walking in the streets are Cuban. The two neighborhoods are only a few meters away from each other, but they are completely different. Despite its tough reputation, Central Havana is a very safe neighborhood and definitely deserves to be explored.

In Central Havana, the streets are almost always packed with people. There will be motorcycles driving beside you, people riding bikes, and cars and trucks slowly chugging along. It might feel like you are in a festival, but really this is just everyday life for this neighborhood. It's noisy, too. Dogs will be barking and people will be talking loudly. Men push carts filled with bread and produce, shouting and singing loudly about their products and prices.

There are hundreds of cheap places to buy fast food in Central Havana and it seems like everybody is selling pizza, sandwiches, coffee, or juice. If you clearly look like a tourist, then it is possible that some locals will approach you to strike up conversations and ask you about your nationality. If you're not in the mood to chat you can just politely say no, and continue walking.

Important Streets

While there are not many clearly defined tourist attractions in Central Havana, there are still plenty of interesting places to see, especially for the traveler looking to explore a little bit off the beaten path. Central Havana is a maze of small, crowded streets. Due to the high population density, it is also a great place to find hundreds of tiny shops and businesses. The following is a summary of some important roads in the neighborhood.

Neptuno Street

Neptuno is probably the busiest street in Central Havana. It starts just two streets north of the Capitolio and winds its way through the neighborhood, passing through some of the most congested shopping areas in the city. Neptuno it is also a major taxi route for travelers going to Vedado. This will be discussed in a later section. Walking along Neptuno can feel hectic but it will also give you a window into the average daily life in the city. Also, there are many street food stands along Neptuno and almost all of the delicious, cheap foods which are discussed in this guide can be found in shops along this street.

Zanja

Starting just south of the Capitolio, **Zanja** runs through the middle of Central Havana. It makes its way through some of the poorest areas of the neighborhood, including the old *Barrio Chino* (Chinatown) district. In recent years, there has been a concerted effort to modernize this area and that can be seen in the clusters of new, higher-end paladares and food stands which are popping up along Zanja street.

Reina (Simón Bolívar)

Starting just south of the Parque Central, which is located beside the Capitolio, is **Reina** Street. It's a mecca for small shops and street vendors, who sell not only food, but also handmade clothes, shoes and household items. Several bazaars and flea markets are located near the eastern end of Reina, which are always interesting to browse. Closer to the Vedado neighborhood this street takes on the name *Carlos Tercero*. While small shops continue to spill onto the sidewalk in this area, the major attraction is the huge, spiral shaped Carlos Tercero shopping center. More information will be provided in the Shopping (p.144) section of this guide.

Avenida de Italia (Galiano)

This is one of the most famous streets in Central Havana. It is lined with large shopping malls as well as a few large discos, clubs, theaters and music halls. Even if you have no desire to shop at all, it is always fun to walk down this perpetually bustling street and see the locals going about their business.

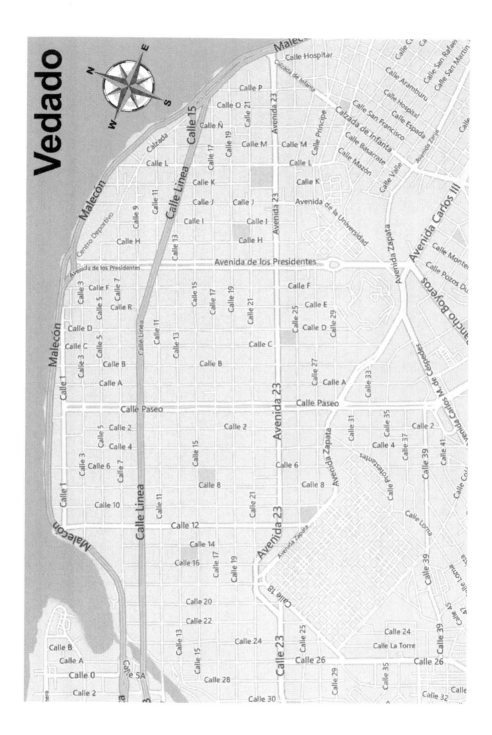

Vedado

Vedado is located west of Central Havana. It is the largest neighborhood in the city and is generally considered the richest. It is peaceful and safe, while still offering a lot of attractions. One of the best things about Vedado is that it is relatively ignored by tourists. Although its popularity has increased markedly over the last years, it is still uncommon to find large gatherings of tourists like you might encounter in Central or Old Havana.

The University of Havana is located in the eastern part of Vedado. This means that there are always lots of young people in the neighborhood and there is a high concentration of cheap restaurants, street food vendors and fun bars and clubs. The main hospitals in the city are also located beside the university.

In the western part of Vedado, there are many government buildings and foreign embassies. This area is generally calmer and quieter, especially at night.

The poorest area of Vedado is located beside the Malecon, where there are many large housing projects. This area is also one of the most interesting because it has many cheap markets, state discount stores and low priced restaurants.

Places of Interest

La Rampa - Also called Calle 23, **La Rampa** is a busy road which cuts across the Vedado neighborhood from east to west. It is the most popular street in Vedado, both for traffic and shopping. It is a main reference line for orienting yourself in the Vedado neighborhood.

El Malecon - The **Malecon** runs along the northern edge of the city but it is busiest in the Vedado neighborhood. During the day, it is a popular meeting spot and a common place for locals to come to relax. Many Cubans also fish and swim in the coastal waters. In the

119

late evening and at night, particularly on weekends, thousands of locals flock to the Malecon, sitting down on the wall and chatting with friends, playing music and drinking. It is a cheap form of entertainment and an excuse to leave the house, especially on hot nights. The main gathering point is near the corner of the Malecon and La Rampa. Even in a city with so many entertainment options, spending a night sitting on the Malecon is still probably the best way to have fun and interact with locals.

Habana Libre Hotel - The **Habana Libre Hotel** is located at the corner of Calle 23 and L. This is one of the busiest intersections in the whole city. The area near this corner is a major traffic hub both for buses and communal taxis. At any time throughout the day, thousands of people are gathered around this area. You will surely find yourself here often if you are going to use public transportation or taxis to explore the city. The large **Cinema Yara** is directly across the street from the hotel and it has a pavilion in front which is a very popular place for young people to congregate and wait for friends. Just on the opposite street corner, there is the massive **Coppelia** ice cream parlor, which occupies almost a whole city block. Hundreds of people are usually lined up all around, waiting for their turn to order. Furthermore, facing the Coppelia there is an immensely popular state-run fast food restaurant named **La Casa del Perro Caliente**. This place specializes in selling jumbo hot dogs and there is always a long lineup of locals in front.

El Edificio Focsa (The Focsa Building) - This is the tallest building in Cuba, and one of the most famous in Havana. **El Focsa**, as the locals call it, is located just a few blocks north of the Habana Libre Hotel, at the intersection of 17 and M. It's important as a landmark, as you can see the giant, green building from most locations in the city. Furthermore, there are some very popular and well stocked shops on the ground floor, including a modern supermarket, a hardware store and a money exchange office (CADECA).

Avenida de Los Presidentes (Calle G) - This is a major north-south route for traffic between the Malecon and the medical campuses located at the southern tip of Vedado. Past this point, the street branches out and changes name, stretching deep into Central Havana. Between **Avenida De Los Presidentes'** four lanes, there is a very wide median with hundreds of benches and ornately trimmed trees. On most days, people come to this area to relax, read or eat lunch. At night, this area really comes alive. It is a popular meeting spot for young people who come to lounge on the benches and relax on the grass, under the trees. At the corner of Calle 23 there is a convenient open air bar which serves up cheap drinks, ensuring that the party goes on late into the night.

Avenida Paseo - This is another major north-south traffic artery located seven blocks west of Ave. de Los Presidentes. **Paseo** bisects the large Vedado neighborhood into two districts. The eastern half is simply named Vedado, and the western district is referred to as **Nuevo Vedado** (New Vedado). At the northern tip of Paseo, near the Malecon, you will find the **Melia Cohiba** and **Riviera** hotels as well as a large shopping mall named **Galerías de Paseo**. At the southern tip of Paseo there is the huge **Jose Marti Memorial** tower and the sprawling **Plaza de la Revolución** square. This area is used to host massive crowds during political rallies and celebrations. It's also a popular tourist destination and the location of the often photographed, 5-story tall, steel outline of the war hero Che Guevara's face, which is mounted on the wall of the Ministry of the Interior building.

Transportation

There are many options for transportation when getting around Havana. The city is not particularly large and most people will be able to walk from Old Havana to Vedado in about 45 minutes. Walking offers you a great opportunity to see the city and meet people, but it might become tiring after a while. Furthermore, if you are only spending a short while in Havana, you might wish to take a faster form of transportation. Public transportation is not very convenient and should probably be avoided. Buses are often very crowded and pass infrequently. Moreover, there are no maps or indications as to where the bus routes begin and end. Even local Cubans are often confused by the organization. The majority of Cubans move around on foot, on bike, or by using a well developed and cheap system of taxis.

Bici Taxis

In Old Havana and Central Havana there are bicycle taxis. These are small, three wheeled vehicles which can seat two passengers in the back, while a Cuban driver pedals in front. *Bici Taxis* are cheap and safe. They are a common form of short distance transportation for both locals and foreigners. Always negotiate the price before starting the trip. To give you an idea, you should be able to get from one end of Old Havana to the other for about 1 CUC.

Coco Taxis

Another form of transportation in Havana is the *Coco Taxi.* These are small, three wheeled, motorized vehicles which seat a driver and two passengers. They are painted bright yellow and look a bit like coconuts on wheels. You can use them to get around or to take a scenic tour of the city. Coco Taxis are noisy and seem less safe than traditional taxi cars, but they are fun and affordable. Expect to pay about 1 CUC per km.

State Taxis

If you are going further and want to get there faster, there are always hundreds of taxi cars on the road which will take you anywhere, very inexpensively. State taxis are painted yellow and black; these will take you from any destination directly to another destination. For example, you can take one from the Capitolio, all the way to the front door of a casa particular in Vedado. That trip might cost 3 CUC. As always, negotiate the price first. If you are a tourist, then you can expect the taxi driver to propose an artificially high price, so you should always negotiate it down substantially. If the driver says 10 CUC, tell him you will pay 3 CUC. If he says 5, just say 3 again.

Within Havana, 3 CUC is more than enough to get you from one end of the city to another. Note: Late at night, prices increase substantially as there are fewer state taxis operating.

Communal Taxis

By far, the cheapest taxi options in Havana are the privately owned taxis called *taxis particulares*. As mentioned earlier, these are the old American cars, from the 1950's or 60's, which are used as communal taxis. These taxis will not drop you off directly at your destination; they simply follow routes, like buses. You can get on and get off at any point along the way. The cost to use these taxis is a flat price of 10 pesos (MN), per person, for any routes inside the city.

Learning to use the taxis particulares will not only improve your understanding of the city and allow you to experience authentic Cuban transportation; it will also **save you tons of money**. I explain the most common taxi routes below, in the section titled Havana Taxi Particular Routes (p. 123).

Interesting Fact: In the city of Havana, state-operated taxis are commonly referred to by locals as *Cinco Cinco* taxis, which means "five five" taxis. They are given this name because the telephone number to reserve a taxi in Havana is 855 5555. As a tourist I would not recommend reserving a state taxi ahead of time, considering it is so easy to find one in almost any location.

Havana Taxi Particular Routes

Getting Around Vedado

If you are not familiar at all with the city, this is the time to take out the map and start following along. The main taxi routes in Vedado run along Calle 23 and Linea. These are two of the busiest streets in Vedado and the taxis on these roads are either going eastward in the direction of Old Havana or westward, toward the suburbs of Miramar, Playa, or La Lisa.

For example: If you are at the corner of 23 and 26th street, and you want to get to the Habana Libre hotel (23 and L), you can basically take any taxi running eastward along 23, as it will at some point pass in front of the hotel. The inverse would also apply. If you are in front of the Coppelia (23 and L) and want to get to get to 23 and 26th street, simply hop into any taxi going west along 23rd street, and it will take you there.

If you are moving along Linea Street, which runs directly parallel to 23, the idea is exactly the same. If your final destination is on Linea, simply take the taxi running in that direction and get off when you are near your destination.

From Vedado to Other Neighborhoods

If you want to get from Vedado to Old Havana, simply hail a taxi running eastward on 23rd Street or Linea and ask the driver if he is going to *La Habana*. Simply stating *La Habana*, as the taxi pulls to the side, is enough to get an answer from the driver. The taxi will either stop and wait for you to get inside, or it will drive off without you. The *La Habana* stop is in front of the Capitolio building.

There are a few main streets in Vedado which run perpendicular to both 23rd and Linea. These streets make it easy to grab a taxi going directly from Vedado to Old Havana, or to catch taxis before they start their route going into and out of Vedado. For example: Taxis traveling east along 23 will almost always turn up O street on their way to Old Havana. Hailing any taxi traveling on O street (it's a one way street) is the easiest way to get to Old Havana. The trip takes about 5 minutes.

L Street is another great way to snag a taxi particular. L Street is parallel to O, but flows in the opposite direction (one way). It is always congested with hundreds of taxis, especially in the area right in front of the Habana Libre Hotel. The taxis on L Street will either be turning on 23rd or Linea, as they continue their westward route.

If you want to travel to the heart of Central Havana, your best bet is to hail a taxi traveling on M Street and ask the driver if he will be going to *Infanta*. Infanta Street bisects the neighborhoods of Vedado and Central Havana and runs through some remarkably interesting areas, filled with eccentric shops and large markets. While taxis going to Infanta Street can be hailed on either 23rd or Linea, the ones traveling along M Street are sure to be going there. The final stop along the Infanta route is usually in the southern suburb of El Cerro. This is one of the poorest neighborhoods of Havana, but it's an interesting place to explore, and is well off the beaten tourist path.

Both Calle G (Ave. de Los Presidentes) and Paseo are north/south running streets with active taxi traffic from the Malecon, through Vedado, and into other neighborhoods. Taxis running south along Calle G will either be going to the Plaza de la Revolución neighborhood, or will turn just on the outskirts and make their way into Central Havana, along Ave. Salvador Allende, which is a popular shopping destination. Taxis traveling along Paseo will pass by the massive Plaza de la Revolución square and the Jose Marti Memorial. These are very popular tourist destinations. They will then continue their route deeper into the Plaza de la Revolución neighborhood.

Central Havana and Old Havana Taxi Routes

The taxis particulares routes in Central and Old Havana are very easy to understand. The de-facto taxi terminal is at the Capitolio, and the Parque Central which surrounds it. Taxis particulares are not permitted in the core Old Havana district, so the closet they can drop you off is in front of the Capitolio. From this location, you only have to walk across Prado Street to get into Old Havana. Conveniently enough, all of the main streets which travel through Central Havana run close to the Capitolio too, so it is very easy to find a taxi that is traveling into Central Havana, or directly to Vedado or any other neighborhood.

At the southern end of the Capitolio are the streets of Dragones (Zanja) and Simón Bolívar (Reina), which travel directly through Central Havana, until Vedado. There is also Maximo Gomez (Monte) street, which travels south into the neighborhood of El Cerro. Taxis are always plentiful along these streets.

Just one block north of the Capitolio, is Neptuno Street. This is a one way, westward-flowing street filled with shops and restaurants. Neptuno is a great street to explore on its own, but it's also a main artery for taxis. All of the taxis on this street are traveling to Vedado, and will either be turning on 23rd or Linea. If your end destination is near either of these streets, simply hail a taxi on Neptuno and ask which street they are taking.

All the streets mentioned above are located beside the Capitolio, but you usually don't even have to walk directly to those specific streets in order to hail a taxi particular. Since most of the taxis pass in front of the Capitolio, on Prado Street, you can simply hail a taxi from that location. Taxis traveling south on Prado will either be turning on Dragones, Simón Bolívar or Maximo Gomez. Taxis traveling north on Prado will almost always be turning on Neptuno. If you want to take any of these streets, just hail a taxi particular in front of the Capitolio and ask them which street they are going to travel along.

Summary

These are the most popular taxi particular routes in the main Havana neighborhoods. There are dozens of other routes which can be useful if you have to get to specific destinations, and those will be discussed throughout this book. The above routes, although they may seem complex at first glance, are actually rather simple to understand once you become a bit familiar with the city. For a novice, sticking with the main Vedado routes of 23rd street or Linea and using Neptuno to travel through Central Havana on your return to Vedado will be the simplest options until you gain confidence to

126

adventure further.

Interesting Fact: A child can ride in a taxi particular for free, as long as they are seated on an adult's lap. Furthermore, for safety reasons, children must always ride in the back seat of a taxi particular, whether they are accompanied by an adult or not.

The Havana Suburbs

The vast majority of tourists will never leave the main Havana neighborhoods of Vedado, Central Havana and Old Havana. This is a shame, because in reality, the Havana suburbs are fantastic places to explore. These suburbs are not sleepy, desolate areas like the bedroom communities that can be found around most western cities. In Havana, the suburbs are filled with people and, in some cases, are even busier than downtown areas. Best of all, in the suburbs you will be immersed in the Cuban lifestyle since there are virtually no foreigners and absolutely no tourist-oriented shops or restaurants.

El Cerro

South of Central Havana and Vedado you will find the large neighborhood of **El Cerro**. The main roads leading to this suburb are the north/south oriented streets of Infanta (in Vedado) and Maximo Gomez (in Central Havana). Continuing even further south you will eventually get into the neighborhood of **Diez Octubre**, and going a bit east from there, the very hilly suburb of **San Miguel del Padron**. If you are in Old Havana you can simply walk, bike, or take a taxi east along Ave. del Puerto, which runs all along the Bay of Havana, and you will pass through all of these neighborhoods. The road concludes on the opposite side of the Bay of Havana, in the town of Regla. The largest attraction in El Cerro might be the Estadio Latinoamericano (corner Ave. 20 de Mayo and Amenidad), which is the stadium where Havana's *Industriales* baseball team plays.

<u>Regla</u>

On the other side of the Bay of Havana, is the town of **Regla**. As mentioned, you can get there by going all the way around the Bay, but there is also a much more direct and cost effective route. Just take the Regla ferry. The ferry terminal is located in Old Havana, at the corner of San Pedro (Ave. del Puerto) and Santa Clara Street, directly in front of the **Catedral Ortodoxa Rusa** (Russian Orthodox Cathedral). The building is unmarked but is easy to identify since it juts out into the harbor and there are always a few security guards in front (you must pass through a metal detector in order to get on the ferry). The ferry costs only 0.2 peso (MN). This is such a small price that most tourists simply pay 1 peso to board, since they do not have smaller change. The ride is noisy but safe, and only takes about 15 minutes. It leaves about every half hour. The town of Regla is not large but it is beautiful, quiet and very clean. Along the main road there are dozens of great places to eat and prices are very cheap.

While the ferry going to Regla is the most popular ferry line, there is also another ferry operating out of the same Havana terminal. Named the **Casablanca** ferry, it will take you across the bay of Havana and drop you off at the Casablanca terminal, about 1 km north of Regla. At this terminal you will find the Hershey Train Station. I will discuss taking this train in more detail in the section titled <u>Riding The Hershey Train</u> (p.172).

<u>Miramar and Playa</u>

Going west from Vedado, you will have to take either a bridge or a tunnel to get into the neighborhoods of **Miramar** and **Playa**. Miramar is a coastal neighborhood filled with many upscale hotels and foreign embassies, located directly west of Vedado. Playa is a more residential neighborhood, located a bit further south from Miramar. Both of these suburbs are relatively rich and are great places to explore, as they offer an interesting way to spend a day outside of the hustle and bustle of urban Havana. You can easily walk to these suburbs from Vedado. At the western tips of both Calzada and Linea streets, there are traffic tunnels with pedestrian sidewalks which lead into Miramar. A few blocks further south, on 11th Street, there is a small, 2 lane bridge leading into Miramar which also has pedestrian sidewalks. Further south, at Calle 23, you will find the large *Puente Almendares* bridge, which leads directly into the Playa neighborhood. There are several main attractions in Miramar, such as the *Acuario Nacional* (National Aquarium), the *Isla de Coco* amusement park, and several popular nightclubs. These will all be discussed in the <u>Entertainment</u> (p.177) section of this guide.

<u>Cojimar, Alamar and Playas del Este</u>

These suburbs are located east of Havana. You can get to them by taking a taxi or bus through the Havana Tunnel located at the northern tip of Old Havana, at the mouth of the Bay of Havana. Note that there is no foot traffic permitted in this tunnel. These areas are a little bit more complicated to get to and explore and I will give more details about how to commute there in the section titled <u>The Wonderful Beaches in Havana</u> (p.168)

Taxi Particular Routes in the suburbs

If you anticipate exploring the suburbs, especially the western suburbs of Miramar and Playa, you must know the taxi particular routes. The routes are not difficult to understand if you follow along with the map below. Just note that the price to use a taxi particular to travel between any of the main Havana neighborhoods and the suburbs is 20 pesos (MN) per person.

If you really like to explore and are eager to experience Havana like a local, I strongly suggest taking a taxi particular into one of the suburbs and getting lost for a few hours. You are unlikely to encounter another foreigner and you will probably learn a lot about daily Cuban life. Perhaps you might also make some friends along the way. And always remember that Cuba is one of the safest countries in the world, so wherever you explore, you will always feel comfortable.

If you do not anticipate visiting these areas, you can skip the next section.

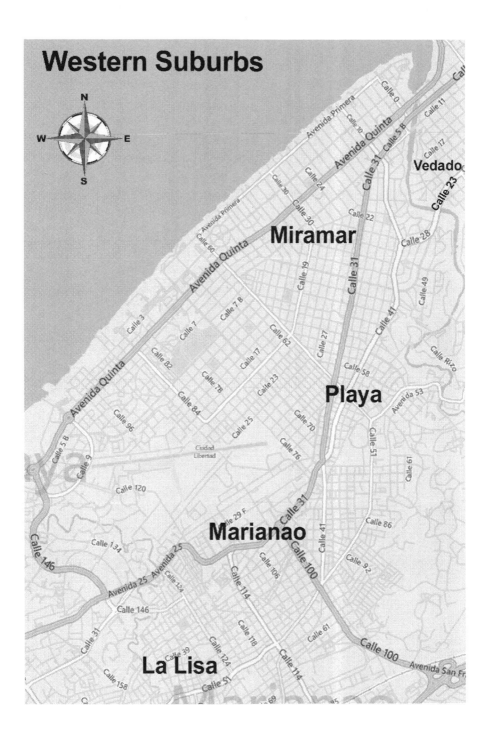

Getting to Miramar

The best way to get from Vedado to Miramar is to simply hail a taxi traveling westward along Linea. Ask the driver if he is going to *Avenida Tercera* (Avenida 3ra), which means 3rd Avenue. This is the main taxi route in Miramar. Avenida 3ra is the main road passing by all the large coastal hotels and most of the popular attractions in the area. The taxis following this route will continue until about 140th Avenue, which is near the end of the Miramar neighborhood. At this point, they will usually turn back east, and start their route again. If you want to use a taxi particular to get from Vedado to the coastal hotels of Miramar or to any of the attractions in this area, this is the route you must take. If you have a particular destination in mind, it is always a good idea to tell the driver in advance. In most cases, he will be able to modify his route in order to drop you off as close to your destination as possible.

Getting to Playa, Marianao or La Lisa

From Vedado, if you want to get to the neighborhoods of **Playa**, **Marianao** or **La Lisa**, you have two options. You can either take a taxi traveling west on Linea or Calle 23. Although both routes are slightly different, they both end in the same place (La Lisa). In order to get to these suburbs, simply hail a taxi traveling west on Linea or Calle 23 and tell the driver which neighborhood you want to go to. The taxi driver will either say yes and stop, or say no and keep driving.

The Linea route runs from Linea Street in Vedado, through the Linea tunnel. It then runs along Ave. 31 (in Playa), then Ave. 41 (in Marianao) and finally Ave. 51 (in La Lisa).

The Calle 23 route is similar. It runs along Calle 23, over the Puente Almendares. It then follows Ave. 41 before merging briefly into Ave. 31, and then making its way to Ave. 51.

<u>Returning from the suburbs</u>

Returning to Havana is very easy. From Playa, Marianao or La Lisa, simply hail a taxi traveling east along one of the main roads (31, 41 or 51) and tell the driver your destination. To get to Vedado, you can either say Linea or Calle 23. For Central or Old Havana, simply say *El Capitolio*.

If you are in Miramar, simply go to Ave. 3ra or Ave. 7ma (7th Avenue). Most taxis traveling east on these streets will go into Vedado, traveling along Linea Street.

Exchanging Money in Havana

If you need to exchange money in Havana, you will have to either use a CADECA exchange office or visit a bank branch. Exchange rates at these locations are virtually identical. There are over 200 CADECA locations in Havana, usually clearly indicated on street signs in front of the offices. Banks in Havana operate under the *Banco Metropolitano* banner. Remember, while banks can exchange foreign currency into CUC, they cannot convert CUC into Moneda Nacional. The only way to get Moneda Nacional is to use a CADECA. For speed and convenience, I always recommend using a CADECA rather than a bank.

Below, I have listed some of the best and easiest to find CADECAs and banks in the Vedado neighborhood.

<u>Ground floor of the Focsa Building:</u> This CADECA is tucked away, under the Focsa building, in the small shopping plaza located on the ground floor. It is not well marked. It is located beside a perfume shop and in front of small toy store. Exchange rates are listed in the window and are usually hand written. There is always a lineup at this location and sometimes the wait can be up to half an hour, especially if you go around lunch time. There are only 2 tellers on duty. Hours of operation: 8am to 5pm, Mon-Sat, and 9am to 1pm on Sunday.

Just around the corner from this CADECA is a Banco Metropolitano where you can also exchange foreign currency into CUC.

23 near the corner of J: This is one of the most popular and prominent CADECAs in Vedado. There are usually 6 or more tellers on duty. There is usually a long lineup, but it tends to flow rapidly. On weekends, service is always slower and you can sometimes wait over 30 minutes. Hours of operation: 8am to 6pm, Monday to Saturday and 9am to 1pm on Sunday.

At the corner of 23 and J, there is a Banco Metropolitano where you can exchange foreign currency into CUC.

19th between A and B: This is a tiny CADECA stand with only 2 tellers located on the western tip of the 19th and B market. There is almost never a lineup at this location; even on busy weekends, service is extremely fast. This location is closed on Mondays. Regular hours of operation are 9am to 4pm, Tuesday to Sunday.

Linea between Paseo and A: The lineups at this location are short and service is usually very fast. Hours of operation: 8am to 5pm, Monday to Saturday and 9am to 1pm on Sunday.

CADECAs in Other Neighborhoods

With over 200 exchange offices in Havana, it's safe to say that you will never be too far away from one. A complete list of all locations would be far too long for this guide. If you are having trouble finding a CADECA as you explore Havana, you should know that most hotels have a small exchange office inside their lobbies. Simply ask at the front desk and they will be happy to point you in the right direction. These offices conveniently operate late into the night; however their exchange rates might be slightly less favorable.

ATMs in Havana

Most of the ATMs in Havana can be found in Old Havana, in the lobbies of large hotels. If you come across a hotel that does not have a functioning ATM, the front desk or doorman will always be able to tell you where the closest one is located.

The CADECA located at 257 Obispo (between Cuba and Aguliar streets), in Old Havana, has an adjacent ATM which operates from 10am to 2am daily. This is one of the most popular exchange offices in the city. But note that, in most cases, it only accepts Visa credit cards for obtaining CUCs. If you have a MasterCard or other credit card, you will need the assistance of a teller and will have to show your passport as identification. The CADECA office is open daily from 8am to 10pm.

Havana by Bike

In my opinion, the best way for a foreigner to explore Havana is by bike. With a bike, you will be able to cover a lot of distance and still have the flexibility to choose your own route and stop to explore wherever and whenever you want, without having to walk all day. Perhaps most importantly, on a bike you will be able to wander without being bothered by locals constantly trying to strike up conversations or offering you taxi rides. Biking in Havana is relatively safe, compared to other large, metropolitan destinations since traffic generally moves slowly and drivers are very careful.

If you are interested in biking around Havana, it is highly advisable to bring your own bike. A simple, inexpensive used bicycle will be perfectly fine. Most airlines permit travelers to transport a bike for free or at a nominal cost. Overall, this will be the most cost effective approach, even if you have to buy a cheap used bicycle specifically for your trip, and then pay a supplemental fee to transport it with you to Cuba.

Rentals

In terms of renting a bike, your options are very limited. While there are locations which offer rental services, most are located in the Miramar neighborhood, close to the foreign embassies. Prices can be very high, often 25 CUC per day or more for a basic bike. Your best option for a bike rental is to simply approach a local with a bike and offer them a bit of money to borrow it for the day. Even if the person declines your offer, they may refer you to somebody else with a bike available. If you are successful, you can usually expect to pay a local about 5 CUC per day for a bike rental. If you are staying at a casa particular, you should also ask your landlord about a bike rental. On rare occasion, they may have a bike or know somebody who does, and might be interested in renting it out.

Buying a Cheap Bike

Buying a bike in Havana is relatively difficult and can be very expensive. Furthermore, the quality of the bikes available, both new and used, is very low. For example, a new bike, purchased at a state store will usually cost at least 120 CUC. It will be a very basic mountain bike and will often require considerable assembly. On the used market, the cheapest adult bikes will be about $40. These bikes will usually be a mishmash of rusted, antiquated parts with worn out tires. Better bikes can be had, but will cost much more.

Nevertheless, if you find yourself in Havana and in need of a bike, your best option may be to pay a bit more for a used bike that is in reasonable condition. The best location to search for a used bike is near the intersection of Maximo Gomez and Manglar streets, in the Central Havana neighborhood, beside the old *Cuatro Caminos* market. Many people walk around this area, promoting used bikes that they are trying to sell. Just a few streets south, at the corner of Vigia and Pila streets, you will find dozens of used bike vendors and bike mechanics. On some weekends there are literally hundreds of old bikes on display in the streets, with mechanics busily working to get them all repaired. This is the only area of Havana where I have

136

consistently seen many bike dealers and actually had any success with purchasing a used bike for a reasonable price.

Note: Several sources on the internet claim that there is a "bike depot" located beside the Capitolio, in the *Edificio Metropolitano.* To my knowledge, this depot no longer exists.

Your other option to buy a used bike is to look on the Cuban classified ads website, Revolico.com. The prices on this site are usually considerably higher, but it is a good opportunity to hone your negotiation skills.

Bike Repairs

If your bike needs repairs, the best place to go is to a local *ponchera* mechanic shop. These tiny, independently run businesses are usually located around gas stations and popular taxi stops. The mechanics specialize in repairing tire punctures for both cars and bikes, but can handle most other small fixes as well. Puncture repairs cost only 10 pesos (MN).Thousands of these shops are scattered around Havana; just look for the sign in front reading *Ponchera.*

Important Note: If you plan on using a bike in Cuba, always remember to bring a good lock with you, since bike locks are almost impossible to find in Cuba and theft is high. Even if you have a good lock, the best way to be absolutely sure that your bike will be safe is to park it in a secure facility, called a *Parqueo.* Throughout Havana, wherever there is a parking lot, you will notice attendants, dressed in state-issued, red and white uniforms, keeping watch over the cars, motorcycles and bikes. For a nominal sum (half a peso (MN) per hour) the attendant will guard your bike. The small cost is well worth the peace of mind.

Common Tourist Scams... Especially in Havana

Unfortunately, due to the stressed economic situation in Cuba and the prevalence of relatively well off, and often naive, tourists, scams perpetrated against foreigners are common. These are mostly minor scams of opportunity which result in the tourist losing only a few dollars. The schemes are self-serving, but never inherently malicious. Nevertheless, you should always be vigilant and aware that the possibility of small time fraud is present. If you are in Cuba for a few days and you clearly look like a tourist (backpack, fair complexion, large camera, speaking any language other than fluent Cuban Spanish), you will likely be approached by a scam artist, or witness another tourist being scammed. Since Havana is the largest, most populous city and has a high concentration of tourists, scams are especially common there. Below I have described some of the most common cons to look out for.

The Helpful Guide

The helpful guide is a friendly stranger who will approach you on the street and strike up a conversation, usually beginning with the line, "Hello my friend," or "Where are you from?" Their goal is to gain your confidence and then offer to show you around the city or escort you to whichever destination you are interested in visiting. If you strike up a friendship, they will usually broaden the scam by telling you a sob story about a sick relative who requires expensive medicine and needs clothes (usually completely false). Their ultimate goal is to get you to buy them a few drinks or a meal, or give them whatever gifts you have brought to Cuba. This is a common scam, and it may cost its victims a few dollars, but it is relatively harmless.

The Best, Cheapest Restaurant in the City

This con requires just a bit more sophistication than the one mentioned above. Usually the approach will be the same - a friendly Cuban greets you and tries to strike up a conversation. After a while, he (these scams are usually perpetrated by men) tells you about a great local restaurant (paladar) which is extremely cheap and offers the best food in the city. Once inside the restaurant, the food and drinks will usually arrive at your table very rapidly, sometimes even before you've seen the menu. At the end of the meal, an outrageously expensive bill is presented to you. The scammer's goal is to rope you into the restaurant and have you eating, drinking and enjoying yourself before you realize that the prices are exaggerated. Usually, the scammer will even eat with you and reassure you that the meal is inexpensive. In return for his effort, the con artist receives a commission from the restaurant, and a free meal. The restaurant prospers by making a huge sale. The tourist is left holding the bag for a lobster dinner and cocktails costing 50 CUC or more. Always check the menu and prices before ordering any meal!

I Never Ordered That!

This is one of the most popular restaurant scams in Cuba, and probably the whole world. After your meal at a restaurant, you receive the tab and there are a few extra items on the bill which you never ordered or ate. It's a very simple scam and preys on the tourist's carelessness and naiveté. Always check your bill at the end of the meal and make sure there are no extra charges for items which you never ordered. This is also a common scam in bars and nightclubs.

That's Extra...

This con is particularly popular in state-run restaurants. The menu will list a series of table d'hôte specials (*ofertas*) which include a main meal, salad, a drink and dessert, all for one low price. When you make your order, the waitress will inform you that the menu has changed, and that those items are no longer included in the table d'hôte, and must be purchased separately. The goal of the scam is for the waitress to get you to buy all the items separately, and then to pocket the difference in price between the individual items and the bargain meal cost. Usually, if you start to complain, the waitress will start talking rapidly, using unintelligible Cuban slang, in an effort to simply get you to agree to order the items separately as she originally suggested. Your only options are to ask to speak with the boss (*El Jefe*) or leave the restaurant and dine at another location. Whatever you do, never acquiesce to the demands of the wait staff. If a state-run restaurant changes a menu offering, **a new menu will always be printed**. Common restaurant workers do not have the authority to change menu prices or offerings. Any claim to the contrary is always false.

The Boss Isn't Here

As a continuation of the above con, if you ever feel you are being mistreated in a restaurant, always ask to see the boss (*El Jefe* (masculine) or *La Jefa* (feminine)). If politely asking does not work, then you might have to be more forceful with your demands. Raise your voice if necessary. **There is always a manager on the premises**. Cuba is one of the most highly bureaucratic countries in the world, a boss, or multiple bosses, will always be on duty. They usually take their jobs more seriously than the regular wait staff and will be much more helpful in resolving your problem. Never accept the excuse that "the boss isn't here." If simply asking to see the boss doesn't work, threaten to leave the restaurant without paying or take down the names and phone numbers of the employees. The boss will soon appear.

Multiple Menus

As mentioned in an earlier section, for all state-operated restaurants, there will only be one menu per establishment. The food will either be priced in CUC or Moneda Nacional. In some cases, the food will be priced in MN while the alcohol will be priced in CUC. This is normal. But, there will never be two completely different menus with different prices. **There are never separate tourist menus and Cuban menus.** If you are ever presented with a menu which looks a bit strange, always check the cover page to see if it is actually the menu for the restaurant you are visiting. A common scam is to mix menus from different restaurants, passing off the higher priced menu in low priced restaurants. This can further be complicated when a restaurant has a disco or separate bar attached to it. While the disco or bar might have a menu priced in CUC, the actual, sit down restaurant might only use Moneda Nacional. The front page of the menu as well as the letterhead, will always clearly indicate which restaurant it is to be used for.

Hand Written Menus

At state owned restaurants, **menus will always be typed** and presented in a professional folder or laminated sheet. State restaurants are operated by large, professionally run, government-owned companies. All prices and menu items are set by official sources. Waitresses or local restaurant managers have no leeway to change or modify food offerings. In a state restaurant, if you are ever presented with a hand written menu, it is a 100% certainty that you are being scammed. Your choice is to either leave the establishment and find another restaurant or to immediately demand to see the manager (*El Jefe*) and hope that the matter can be resolved. If you have a camera in your possession, I would suggest that you snap a photo of the hand written menu as proof of your complaint, because it will likely disappear without a trace by the time the manager arrives.

Note about scams: Far and away, the most common small scams occur in restaurants and bars when tourists are distracted and not paying attention to the menu or bill. I have mentioned the most common scams, but this list is by no means exhaustive. As long as you pay attention and realize that you can always demand to speak to the restaurant manager or boss if there is any major discrepancy, you will be fine. In Cuba, **the tourist is king**. The Cuban economy is completely reliant on tourism and the goal of all state-run companies is to encourage tourist enjoyment and repeat business. If you ever think you are being conned and feel you have no other alternatives, simply threaten to call the police or the authorities. This will usually put a quick halt to the scam. If the scammer ever threatens to call the police on you, for example, if you refuse to pay an obviously inflated restaurant bill, never have any fear. Even if the police were to come to investigate the situation (highly unlikely), they will always take the side of the tourist over the restaurant, simply to defuse the situation and end the conflict.

Interesting Fact: Most scams are perpetrated by individual, small time con artists. Their main goal is to make a few dollars per day, as this would equate to a very high salary by Cuban standards. Larger crimes or robberies are very rare in Cuba.

Resort and Hotel Scams

Hotels and large resorts are generally extremely safe. Although common sense precautions should always be taken, it is unlikely that any of your personal possessions will ever be stolen by the staff at these establishments. Hospitality jobs are some of the most highly prized and best paying forms of employment in the country; no worker would risk their job to steal a few dollars from a tourist.

Your biggest threat in the resort is usually from other guests. They are the most likely to pocket unattended cameras or cell phones. Furthermore, it is common to encounter theft problems at resorts which charge a deposit fee to use beach towels. Tourists who misplace their borrowed towels often simply steal a replacement from another guest. Inevitably, the finger of blame gets pointed at the staff. The only way to prevent such theft is to always keep a close eye on your belongings.

Living Cheaply in Havana

Budgeting

Obviously, budgets can vary dramatically from one person to the next. The Cuban government recommends that all tourists entering the country have with them at least the equivalent of $100 USD per person, per day of their stay. I would recommend that you bring approximately this much currency with you as well. This will help you to avoid any problems, and to ensure that you have enough money for any foreseeable situation. If you have a credit or debit card, and are certain that it will function in Cuba, you can bring it as well, in place of some of the hard currency. Nevertheless, I recommend bringing a good supply of cash, so you can easily convert some to CUC, rather than having to search for an ATM immediately upon arriving in Cuba.

Accommodations - You should factor spending about 20 to 30 CUC per night for a casa particular. Hotels can be more expensive. If you are staying longer than 2 weeks, you should be able to negotiate the nightly rate considerably.

Food - You can easily get by with eating cheap and readily available food sold at street side shops. Estimate about 10 to 20 pesos (MN) per sandwich or small meal. This equates to about 2 to 3 CUC per day. For a more healthy approach, you might consider having a larger evening meal in a restaurant. Under this plan you might expect to spend a total of 5 to 6 CUC per day on food.

Alcohol - This category is highly dependent on the individual. Estimate that most cans of beers cost 1 CUC or less.

Transportation - You can easily walk around most of the city. Although this is time consuming, it is great exercise and the best way to meet locals and learn the culture. If you anticipate using taxis particulares a few times per day, budget to spend about 50 pesos (MN) or 2 CUC daily. For state taxis, estimate 5 to 6 CUC daily.

Entertainment - If the ideas presented in this guide appeal to you, then you should be able to find a great deal of fun in Havana for next to nothing. If you plan to dance the night away in bars and discos, estimate spending an additional 10 to 20 CUC per evening.

Average Budgets:

Cheap: If you are budget conscious and traveling solo, you can expect to spend about 30 to 40 CUC or less, per day. A couple can easily get by with 50 CUC per day (25 CUC each). This includes the price for accommodations at an inexpensive casa particular.

Moderate: If you want to live like a local Cuban while also enjoying a few extravagances per day, such as having a few more drinks, staying at a fancier casa, and making greater use of taxis, you can expect to spend about 50 CUC per day (solo) or about 70 CUC for a couple (35 CUC each).

High: If you really want to go all out, by renting a luxury casa or hotel room, exclusively using state taxis, eating fancy dinners, and partying late into the night at discos, you can expect to pay considerably more; likely at least 100 to 150 CUC per person, per day. Compared to many other travel destinations, this is still relatively cheap.

Shopping

Shopping in Havana can be a daunting experience. Cuba is not really a place known for its product selections or low prices. I suggest you try to bring everything you anticipate needing for your trip, especially any specialized products. In Cuba, these same items will either be impossible to find, or sold at a price much higher than you would expect.

On the other hand, it is fun to browse inside stores, as the atmosphere is usually quite busy and some of the products on sale are rather unique. Some stores even have small consignment sections which offer a selection of used products at discount prices. Browsing is a great, free way to casually learn a bit about regular Cuban life and provides a glimpse into the budding Cuban economy.

In Havana, there are many state-run department stores, usually operating under the *TRD*, *Panamericana* or *Coral* brand names. They offer a selection of widely used household products as well as clothing, electronics and packaged foods. It is common to find several of these stores grouped together in popular shopping districts and malls. The prices and product selection will vary subtly from one location to the next.

Here is a list of a few popular shopping districts in Havana:

Vedado: There are three main shopping areas in Vedado which have clusters of state stores as well as independently run boutiques.

Calle 23, between Paseo and 10th: There is a cluster of state-run stores selling household goods in both Moneda Nacional and CUC. At the corner of 23rd and 10th there is a former Woolworth's store selling food and household goods, all in Moneda Nacional. Between 8th and 10th, on the north side of Calle 23, there is an independent consignment shop, selling a variety of new and used items.

Ground floor of the Focsa and the Habana Libre Hotel: There is a shopping mall under the Focsa building which includes a hardware store, shoe store and several kid's boutiques. There is also a well stocked supermarket which is very popular. On the ground level of the Habana Libre Hotel there are shops selling cigars, alcohol and clothing. Inside the hotel, on the first floor, there is a galleria with higher end boutiques. At both the Focsa and the Habana Libre, all prices are in CUC.

<u>Galerias Paseo:</u> Located at the corner of Paseo and the Malecon, directly in front of the Melia Cohiba hotel, this large shopping center has a wide selection of goods priced in CUC. The ground floor has a hardware store as well as several restaurants and bars. The second floor has a large supermarket with slightly lower prices than most other supermarkets in Vedado. There are several other stores which sell household goods, furniture and electronics.

Central Havana: There are five main shopping areas in Central Havana.

<u>Plaza Carlos Tercero:</u> Located at the corner of Ave. Salvador Allende (Carlos Tercero) and Arbol, this massive, spiral-shaped shopping center has hundreds of stores and boutiques selling almost everything imaginable. From food to electronics, chocolate to pottery, this is definitely a great place to spend an afternoon browsing. Prices are in CUC, but are reasonable. Note that on the weekend this place is packed with thousands of shoppers.

<u>Avenida de Italia, near Neptuno:</u> There is a dense concentration of stores in this area with products priced both in CUC and Moneda Nacional. You will find the *La Epoca* shopping center which sells jewelry, perfumes and clothing. Beside it is the massive *TRASVAL* hardware store. All along Ave. de Italia, from the Malecon until Zanja, you will find other, smaller state stores selling household goods and clothing in Moneda Nacional. The prices are usually very cheap, although the selection is slim. There are also a few flea markets in the area selling leather goods and shoes at very low prices.

<u>Around the Capitol Building:</u> Here you will find an abundance of high end boutiques selling western branded clothes at exorbitant prices. These stores are generally located on the ground floor of the many luxury hotels surrounding the Capitol building. Nestled between boutiques are dozens of small, Cuban-oriented stores selling basic household goods and clothing in Moneda Nacional. The mix of goods sold at these locations changes on a weekly basis and there

can sometimes be long lineups just to enter. There are also lots of indoor flea markets and independent vendors selling all sorts of products. Tools, jewelry, shoes, clothing, bike parts and piñatas; the selection can be overwhelming, as can the crowds of shoppers flooding these locations.

San Lazaro and Infanta: Both of these streets have high concentrations of state stores and independently run shops. This area is right on the border between Vedado and Central Havana and within walking distance to the University of Havana. There are several large supermarkets, a hardware store and a building materials depot. Many small vendors sell inexpensive, hand-crafted items and jewelry from their front door steps.

Reina: Hundreds of tiny shops line this street as well as a large number of independent clothing vendors. Over the last few years, Reina has developed into a major shopping hub; the street really gets active near the corner of Ave. de Italia. Here you will find the massive *Almacenes Ultra* store. This is one of the largest department stores in the city, spanning over 4 floors of shopping area. Just beside it there is a well stocked hardware store and a leather goods shop. The old Sears Roebuck store is located at the corner of Reina and Amistad, just south of the Capitolio, overlooking the Parque Central. The first floor is now a shoe store.

Old Havana: There are tons of stores in Old Havana, but beware that prices at these locations can be considerably higher than stores just a couple of blocks west, in Central Havana.

Obispo: Havana's most famous shopping street. It is lined with hundreds of high end boutiques, artisanal shops and restaurants. From morning till night, Obispo is packed with thousands of tourists and locals. The prices are very high, even by western standards. Local Cubans almost never shop in this area, but some do congregate along this street, hoping to glean a bit of money from the tourists either by offering taxi rides, guided tours or other services.

<u>San Rafael</u>: Prices are a little bit more reasonable and the shopping atmosphere is more relaxed. While there are some higher end stores, there are also many locations selling goods in Moneda Nacional. San Rafael's wide, cobblestone paved street provides a relaxing environment for an evening stroll and it's a good street for casual window shopping or browsing.

Suburbs: Most tourists will not venture out into the Havana suburbs, especially not for shopping. However, it is important to note a couple of specific areas which are not too far from the city and which offer good shopping experiences.

<u>Mercado Cuatro Caminos</u>: This massive indoor market is located at the corner of Maximo Gomez and Ave. Manglar. This is in the northeast corner of the El Cerro neighborhood, bordering on Central Havana. The *Cuatro Caminos* market was technically closed in February 2014; however there is still a lot of commercial activity in the surrounding area. As mentioned earlier, a few blocks south, near the corner of Vigia and Pila streets, there is a large concentration of bicycle sellers and mechanics.

<u>La Puntilla Shopping Center</u>: Located in Miramar, at the intersection of Calle A and Avenida 1ra, just past the Calzada Tunnel leading out of Vedado. This large shopping center offers a huge selection of goods. Do not let its location deter you from visiting. It's within easy walking distance of Vedado. Prices are in CUC, and don't expect to find bargains, but the selection of goods offered in the grocery and household goods departments far outstrips that of most other locations in Havana. If you want to get there by state taxi, it should cost no more than 3 CUC, leaving from anywhere in Vedado.

<u>Interesting Fact</u>: In many cases, you must check your handbags before entering stores in Cuba. This is an easy and safe process. There will always be a *guardabolsa* (bag watcher) stand located beside or inside state stores. Simply deposit your bags and a clerk will hand you a numbered stub as a claim slip. Sometimes you will be asked to leave your name or a piece of ID. This is so you can

retrieve your bag even if you lose your claim stub. This service is free, but a tiny tip (a peso or a few centavos) is always appreciated.

Markets and Venta Libre Stores

By far, the most common place you will go to shop for your daily consumables will be the markets (agropecuarios) and the state-run *venta libre* stores.

Centro Habana: Markets and venta libre stands are very easy to find. Given the high population density, it is common to find a small market or well stocked fruit stand every few street corners.

Vedado: Small markets, located at street corners, are very common. Moreover, there are some large agropecuario markets which have dozens of stands and sellers, carrying a more varied assortment of fruits, vegetables and meats at lower prices. I have listed a few of these prime locations below.

Smaller Markets:

Corner 27 and E: Small market with 3 or 4 sellers. Prices are reasonable but selection is low. Across the street, between D and E, there is a small but well stocked venta libre stand selling bulk spaghetti, meat, packaged hot dogs, flour and sugar. Prices are low, ranging from 10 to 30 pesos (MN) per pound depending on the product. Sometimes this stand also sells cheese, which is very popular and tends to sell out quickly.

Corner 21 and I: Small market with 3 or 4 sellers. Prices are average but selection is low. There is a meat stand, too.

Corner 25 and I: This market only has 1 or 2 sellers during the week, but up to 7 or 8 sellers on a nice weekend. Prices are lower than average.

<u>Corner 9 and F:</u> This small market is located in one of the poorest sections of Vedado. Prices are cheaper than average. There is also a fresh squeezed juice stand selling most juices for only 2 pesos (MN) per cup.

<u>Corner 9 and I:</u> Another small market located in the same area as the one just mentioned. This poor area has a high concentration of cheap markets and state-run cafeterias serving low priced food.

Larger Markets:

<u>Corner of 17 and K:</u> This is one of the largest open air markets in Vedado, located just a block away from the Focsa building. There are dozens of produce sellers with a good selection of items. Prices are among the lowest in Vedado. In addition to produce stands, there are a few fast food vendors and a couple of butcher shops. At the back of the market there is a *panaderia* and a large venta libre depot with a nice selection of goods.

<u>Corner 19 and B:</u> This is a large, covered market. There are dozens of produce sellers and several butcher stands. There is also a large venta libre depot on the ground floor. Prices at this market tend to be a bit higher than average, likely because this neighborhood is a bit more upscale. There is a very convenient CADECA money exchange office at the western end of the market which almost never has a line-up.

<u>17, between F and G:</u> This is a medium-sized market with about a dozen sellers. Prices are low. A state-run cafeteria located near the entrance to the market sells a variety of low priced, prepared food.

<u>Corner 27 and A:</u> This is a large market with over a dozen vendors. Prices are low. When in season, a stand at this market sells freshly pressed mango and guayaba juice. Across the street from this market, on 27th, there is a *panaderia* and butcher shop.

<u>Tulipan market (Corner Tulipan and Marino streets, Plaza, Havana)</u>

The Tulipan market is located in the Plaza de la Revolucion neighborhood. As the name suggests, this neighborhood is located beside the Plaza de la Revolucion, just south of Vedado. It is one of the largest and most famous markets in Havana. Locals from all over Havana have been known to travel by bus, from across town, just to go to this market. The prices are generally cheaper than markets in Vedado and the high number of independent vendors ensures that the produce is high quality. The market also has a few dedicated Carnicerías (butcher shops) which have been able to grow their business to the point where they have refrigerated display cases to keep the meats fresh. In addition, the market boasts a wide range of independent fast food sellers and mini restaurants. These are especially popular in the morning hours. It is common to see government workers, in official work attire, having breakfast at these paladares in the morning, just before walking to their ministerial jobs in the many office buildings beside the Plaza. The largest paladar in the market is called El Ranchon. It's a newly built, wood beam, open air restaurant with seating capacity for about 30 people. Lunch meals can be had for about 1 CUC. If you find yourself in the area, it's a good place to stop for a quick bite or a fresh juice.

<u>Note:</u> These are just a few of the markets you will find in the city. There are literally thousands more and, in most cases, it would be hard to walk for more than 5 minutes without seeing one. Explore Havana like a local and you will find your own favorite places to shop.

Internet Access Points

Almost all large hotels will offer computer terminals with internet access or WIFI internet. The most important thing to remember when using a terminal or WIFI is to log-out of your internet account at the end of the session. This is especially important for WIFI users. If you don't log out of the WIFI server, you will continue consuming your minutes even after you stop using your computer. Each access point has a different log-out procedure, so check with the technician on duty before you log on.

Typical internet speeds in most hotels will be comparable to 3mbs bandwidth rates, which is reasonably fast, but may not be fast enough for online movie streaming or VOIP internet-based phone calls.

Below I have listed some of the most popular internet access points in Havana. The list is ranked from lowest WIFI internet prices to highest. Note, however, that these prices can and do change often, so always confirm the price before you purchase access time.

Hotel Presidente (Corner G and Calzada (7th) - Vedado)
The internet services area is locate in the main lobby, to the right of the reception desk. There are about half a dozen terminals in good condition. The price to use the internet is 4.50 CUC per hour regardless if you use a terminal or WIFI. To log out, you must type 1.1.1.1 in your browser's address bar. WIFI cards expire thirty (30) days after purchase. Note: Management sometimes refuses to sell access cards to people who are not guests at the hotel. This policy is randomly enforced.

Hotel Nacional (Corner 21 and O - Vedado)
Internet is available at the computer terminals in the business center for the price of 10 CUC per hour. WIFI access is also available at the cost of 7 CUC per hour or 10 CUC for 2 hours.

Hotel Vedado (O between 23 and 25 - Vedado)
Internet time can be purchased in the business center. The price to use the internet via computer terminal or WIFI is the same - 6 CUC per hour or 3 CUC per half hour.

Hotel Melia Cohiba (Corner Paseo and 3 - Vedado)
The internet room is located at the back of the lobby, to the left of the reception desk. There are about a dozen terminals in fair condition. Internet speed feels slightly slower than at some other

locations. The price to use the internet at a computer terminal is 10 CUC per hour. WIFI is also available throughout the lobby and first floor of the hotel at a price of 14 CUC for 2 hours.

Habana Libre Hotel (Corner 23 and L - Vedado)
The internet room is on the second floor atrium. Just walk up the wooden staircase in the lobby and turn left. There are more than a dozen computer terminals available. Their condition is good. The price is 10 CUC per hour regardless if you use a terminal or WIFI. WIFI cards expire three (3) days after purchase, regardless if you use all your time or not.

Hotel Telégrafo (408 Prado at the corner of Neptuno - Old Havana)
Internet is available at the computer terminals located in the business center. The price for usage is 6 CUC per hour. There is no WIFI available in this hotel.

Hotel Inglaterra (416 Prado at the corner of San Rafael - Old Havana)
Internet is available at the computer terminals located in the business center. The price for usage is 6 CUC per hour or 3 CUC per half hour. There is no WIFI available in this hotel.

Hotel Riviera (Corner Paseo/ 3 - Vedado)
Internet is available at the computer terminals located in the business center. The price for usage is 8 CUC per hour. There is no WIFI available in this hotel.

Public WIFI Zones in Havana

In 2015 the Cuban government opened a network of public WIFI spots throughout the island. In Havana the largest WIFI zone is located in Vedado, on 23rd street, stretching from the Habana Libre hotel to the waterfront. There is also another spot located in the park at the corner of Galiano and San Rafael street in Central Havana. To access the WIFI in these locations, you must have a WIFI card with a valid password and pin. As a foreigner, you can purchase the WIFI cards at any ETECSA office (usually there is one beside the WIFI zone). The cards cost 1.50 CUC for 1 hour of usage and you must show identification in order to purchase. Also, beside the WIFI spots you will always find many residents reselling their WIFI access cards at a small markup. Resellers usually charge 2 to 3 CUC per 1 hour card. To access the internet, simply connect to the WIFI and sign in with your code and pin number, as stated on the card. The internet connection is not very fast, but good enough for checking emails and catching up on some news.

Street Food Stands

You will see street food vendors everywhere in Havana and I've mentioned them a lot in this guide. These small, independently run stands sell quick snacks and food at very affordable prices. The easiest way to tell which ones are selling the best food at the best price is to just look for a long lineup in front. The locals always know which vendors are better than the rest.

The sheer quantity of these food stands throughout the city and the fact that individual locations tend to change operators and menu selections so often, makes it impossible to rate these places or to recommend any particular one. Throughout this guide, I have mentioned some streets and areas which are notable for their concentration of good food stands, but I urge you to be adventurous and try eating from any place that looks enticing to you. You will surely find your own favorites.

The following is a short, non exhaustive list of some of the types of foods you will see offered at these street stands.

Sandwiches

These are probably the most popular items. Small sandwiches will have the word *pan* (small bread loaf) in front of their names. For example, a *pan con tortilla* means a small omelet sandwich. A *pan con bistec* refers to a fried pork filet sandwich. The name *sandwich* is usually reserved for a large, triangular wedge of crusty bread, filled with sliced ham, cheese and sometimes cucumber. The smaller version of this would simply be called a *pan con jamon y queso*. In Havana, most food stands will sell large sandwiches for about 10 pesos (MN) or less. Smaller *pan* sandwiches cost about 5 to 6 pesos (MN). *Pan con tortillas* are usually cheaper and can be had for as little as 2 pesos (MN) at some low-cost state cafeterias.

Pan Con Lechon

Perhaps one of the tastiest, cheapest and most authentic Cuban street foods. Although popular with locals, it is generally overlooked by tourists. This will surely change as awareness grows. *Pan con lechon* is a small sandwich filled with thin slices of roasted pork. A tangy garlic sauce, called *mojo*, is drizzled over the meat. Some vendors will even add a slice of tomato, lettuce or cucumber. These sandwiches are not large, but at only 5 pesos (MN) a pop, they are very inexpensive. The best thing about this meal is that the pork is always fresh and the sandwiches are prepared before your eyes. You can see the quality of the ingredients before you purchase.

Hamburgers

While not authentically Cuban, the popularity of hamburgers is universal. In Cuba, most *hamburguesas* are made, fittingly enough, with ground pork meat. Some of the finer street side establishments will even mix in a bit of chorizo sausage, grill the buns in a panini press, or garnish the burger with lettuce, tomato and cheese. In Havana, prices range from 8 to 10 pesos (MN). In my experience, the best burger locations are around the Capitolio. They serve the tastiest and cheapest burgers, grilled fresh to order.

Note: Some state cafeterias will advertise cheap hamburgers, sometimes for as low as 4 pesos. These are not quality burgers, as the meat is usually nothing more than a thin slice of breaded pork croquette. You are better off paying a few pesos more and ordering from an establishment where you can see the burgers being prepared and cooked as you wait.

Hot Dogs

These are most often sold at state-run, fast food outlets, usually in jumbo format. They are called *perros calientes*. Steam cooked and served in large Cuban bread rolls, these usually cost only 10 pesos (MN). Some independent vendors sell them as well, but beware; the cheaper priced ones usually consist of regular sized hot dogs, rather than jumbo ones.

Pizza and Spaghetti

In Cuba, it is almost impossible to find classic, Italian-style pizza and spaghetti. But that's not necessarily a bad thing. The Cuban versions are usually tasty, and at 5 to 10 pesos (MN) per serving, they are definitely affordable. Pizzas are usually prepared in shallow pans and cooked in ovens or barbeques. The dough is usually thick, with crispy, burnt cheese around the edge. *Napoletana* style pizzas are the most popular and are topped with tomato sauce and cheese. Other toppings, such as ham, onion or pineapple can be added at a nominal cost. As for the spaghetti, the serving portions are usually ample, and the tomato sauce and cheese tasty, but the noodles themselves are usually overcooked. If you're a perfectionist, this might disappoint you, but for most, it will not be a major concern.

Cajitas

Another popular fast food option, especially for people desiring a full meal, are small, takeaway cardboard boxes filled with freshly cooked, authentic Cuban food. These little boxes are called *cajitas*. They contain a portion of meat (usually fried pork fillet (*bistec*), a pork chop (*chuleta*), or a battered and fried chicken thigh (*pollo*)), along with rice and beans, a small salad and a side of yuca or sweet potato. In Havana, a cajita will usually cost about 25 to 35 pesos (MN).

Frituras

If you have a hankering for a savory, freshly fried snack, then these will definitely appeal to you. They are little balls of dough, infused with garlic and salt, fried fresh as you order. They cost only 1 peso (MN) each. They come out of the fryer steaming hot, usually still crackling from the boiling oil. It is common to see *fritura* vendors with long lineups in front. Cubans usually order a dozen at a time. Sometimes you might find vendors selling *frituras* made with *malanga*, which is a traditional Cuban root vegetable similar to potato. These are delicious and you should definitely try them.

Meat Croquettes

Croquetas consist of balls of meat, usually of questionable origin, heavily mixed with bread, potato and other filler items. They are then deep fried. Despite their cheap price, usually only 2 pesos (MN) each, most Cubans consider them to be rather unsavory and unhealthy. I would have to agree. This is probably the only street food I would not recommend.

Ice Cream and other snacks

Cubans love their ice cream. In Havana, it will be difficult to walk a block without encountering at least one ice cream vendor. Ice cream is usually sold in cones (*barquillos*) costing 3 pesos (MN) each. Flavors range from the basic vanilla and chocolate to the more exotic flavors of *naranja-pina* (orange-pineapple) and *mantecado* (French vanilla with cinnamon). A cheaper frozen dessert, named *frozzen,* is similar to a soft serve ice cream, but with a lower cream content. Cones come in a variety of flavors and usually cost only 1 peso (MN).

Donuts, called *rosquillas*, are another popular street food dessert. They are usually large, moist, and covered in raw sugar. Some vendors even dip them in honey. In Havana, they usually cost 2 to 3 pesos (MN) each.

Cangrejitos are another common type of pastry, popular as a breakfast or snack. They are crescent-shaped, fried dough puffs, filled with either sweet *guayaba* paste or cheese, They get their name from their crab-like shape and size (*cangrejito* means little crab). In Havana, thcy usually cost 2 to 3 pesos (MN). They are best eaten warm, fresh out of the fryer.

Fruit Drinks

I sometimes get the impression that drinking fruit juice is more popular than water in Havana. If the street vendors are any indication, I might be right. Almost every food vendor will be offering some form of juice to compliment their food selections. Cold, freshly made mango, orange and pineapple juices are popular choices, and usually costs 3 pesos (MN) per cup. These natural juices are called *jugos naturales*. Some vendors choose to sell cheaper options made from water and artificial juice mixes. These are simply called *refrescos* (refreshments) and cost only 1 peso per cup.

Note: Some vendors will water down their fresh squeezed juices. They are still natural, but not as fulfilling as pure juice. Through trial and error, and by watching the buying habits of the local Cubans, you will quickly learn which vendors offer the best products.

Peanut Products

In Cuba, peanuts are called *maní*. They are a very popular snack food. Brigades of independent street vendors, called *maniceros*, roam the streets, selling roasted peanuts, packaged in small paper cones. They especially congregate near bus stops, schools, and outdoor bars. These roasted peanuts cost only 1 peso (MN) per cone (larger cones cost more). *Maní molido*, a type of sweetened peanut butter, is another popular snack. It is sold almost everywhere, packaged in small, wax paper wrapped bars. Prices range from 3 to 12 pesos (MN) per bar, depending on size.

Popular and Cheap Restaurants

There are thousands of great restaurants in Havana. Walk around for five minutes and you are sure to find a good one. Despite what some guidebooks might say, the average quality of food in Havana, especially the authentic Cuban cuisine, is extremely high. As mentioned before, the core meals consist of rice, beans, chicken and pork. Despite the simple ingredients, these meals are very flavorful and filling.

The following list includes some of the cheapest restaurants in Havana. These are locations where you can have a full course, sit down meal for under 5 CUC per person. You will immediately notice that most of these restaurants are located in Vedado. The reason is simple; in Vedado, most of the people eating in restaurants are local Cubans, so the prices are always much lower than restaurants in Old Havana or Central Havana. Furthermore, many of the restaurants on this list are state-run. As outlined earlier, these restaurants often sell the same quality of food you will get at an independent paladar location, but at a much lower cost. Service is sometimes less refined at state restaurants, but that is not a major concern for most people.

Also note that, while these restaurants are cheap, their menus do include some fancier and higher priced items as well. I generally recommend selecting from table d'hôte (*ofertas*) selections as these options are the most popular, freshest and cheapest. The *ofertas* consist of full course meals where there is a main meat dish, as well as side orders of rice, beans, salad and *vianda* (starchy root vegetable like potato or yucca). The meals usually also include a dessert and a drink.

El Carmelo (23 at the corner of H)

This is probably Vedado's best known, fancy, sit down restaurant - but don't let that scare you. While the ambiance is upscale, the prices at this state restaurant are low. All the *ofertas* are priced at less than 5 CUC. They included a main dish with your choice of meat, as well as rice, salad and *vianda*. A drink, either fresh juice or a beer, and a dessert are also included. Portions at this restaurant are huge. The *bistec de cerdo* (fried pork fillet) or the *escalopes de cerdo* (breaded pork fillet) are massive and can easily feed two people. On the regular menu, the pizzas are inexpensive, but nothing to write home about, and while the lasagna is far from being authentic Italian, you get a massive serving, weighing almost 2 pounds and costing only 2.50 CUC. It's easy to see why locals love eating at this restaurant and it will easily make its way into your dining rotation while in Vedado. The restaurant's theme is based around Charlie Chaplin and the classic silent movie era. There is live music on the weekends and even a rather talented Chaplin impersonator, who greets guests (silently) and provides entertainment. All prices are in CUC.

Castillo de Jagua (23 at the corner of G)

Just a block away from El Carmelo, at the corner of 23 and G, stands the very famous Castillo de Jagua restaurant. It was recently reopened after undergoing major renovations. This state-run restaurant is slightly less upscale than El Carmelo, but the portions are of similar size and prices are even cheaper. All food items are priced in Moneda Nacional, but the alcoholic drinks are priced in CUC. The average meal at this restaurant will cost less than 60 pesos (MN) and it would be perfectly reasonable for two people to dine for less than 100 pesos (MN), tip included. The only real downside to this restaurant is that it tends to fill up pretty quickly. If you don't want to wait in line, I suggest arriving before 7pm. Note: I will issue one warning for tourists visiting this restaurant: In the past there have been some instances of the servers handing out menus priced in CUC. Do not be fooled by this scam. In the restaurant, all items are priced only in Moneda Nacional. The CUC menu is exclusively reserved for the small nightclub which is attached to the restaurant. If you have any problems, insist on seeing the Moneda Nacional menu, or speak directly with the manager.

El Cochinito (23 between H and I)

El Cochinito is Spanish for *the piglet*. It's a fitting name because the menu centers around pork dishes, although there are a few chicken items, too. Among locals, this state-run restaurant has developed a bit of a bad reputation, not because of the food quality, but because of the slow service. Honestly, I have dined here many times, and sometimes the service is fast and courteous, and sometimes it takes forever to eat. Regardless, the food is good and the prices are among the cheapest in Havana. *Oferta* specials start at just 30 pesos (MN). This price does not include a drink. Portions are a bit smaller than average, but even if you order extra items, it will probably be very difficult to spend more than 60 pesos (MN) per person for a meal. The restaurant tends to pack up in the evening, but even so, there is rarely a lineup in front. I suggest arriving around 8pm, which is the busy time. Service will actually be a bit faster, as this will be the period when all the staff is working.

Buona Sera (23 at the corner of I)

While this is not a fancy restaurant, it is very popular with locals, and extremely cheap. It's located just down the road from the University of Havana, so it's a popular spot for young people to meet up. The menu of this state-run restaurant is composed of Italian dishes. The food is comparable to Italian dishes you will find throughout Havana. Everything is priced in Moneda Nacional. Prices for a regular cheese pizza (Napoletana) start at only 10 pesos. The price for spaghetti ranges from 10 pesos for a cheese and tomato sauce dish, to 15 pesos for spaghetti garnished with chopped ham. Juices and soft drinks are sold at state prices - soft drink cans are 10 pesos, beers are 18 to 20 pesos depending on brand. Service tends to be a bit slow. For a cheap and simple meal, this is definitely the place to come.

Cinecittà (23 at the corner of 12th)

Named after the famous Roman film studio, the theme of this state-run restaurant is the cinema. The walls are plastered with vintage movie posters and photos of famous actors. This restaurant is located slightly further away from downtown Vedado. Given its location, you will notice very few tourists here. The menu centers around Italian dishes and is very similar to Buona Sera, although more upscale. Everything is priced in Moneda Nacional. Pizza and spaghetti plates start at 10 pesos and lasagna and cannelloni dishes are priced at 25 pesos. Beers and soft drinks are sold at state prices. Ice cream is available as a dessert and costs only 3 pesos per scoop. This restaurant is very popular with young people and the lineups on weekends are notoriously long. During the week, if you arrive before 8pm, there should be no lineup at all. The service at this restaurant is surprisingly fast and the servers are very courteous.

Cafe TV (Calle N, between 17 and 19 - Focsa Building Ground level)

This state-run restaurant is tucked away on the ground floor of the Focsa building. Surprisingly, while most Havana natives have heard about this place, very few actually go to it. Even on a weekend night, this restaurant will be almost empty. There really is no good reason for it. The service is rapid and courteous. The atmosphere, with its television studio theme, is clean and modern. The food is of high quality and surprisingly cheap. All the ofertas are priced under 5CUC and include side dishes and a beer. Portions are very large. It's very likely that once more people discover this location, its popularity will surge. All menu items are priced in CUC. On weekends there is often live entertainment.

<u>Union Francesa de Cuba (Calle 17 at the corner of 6)</u>

This is an upscale, state-run restaurant with a French theme. The dishes are mostly Cuban, but they are prepared and presented with a French flair. It's a delicious combination, and the selection of foods is almost unheard of for a restaurant in Cuba. From pork chops covered in thick French sauces, to filet mignon, grilled fish, and fried shrimp platters, this restaurant will definitely impress. Prices are all in CUC, and although they might be slightly higher than average, they are still reasonable for the portions you receive. Expect to pay about 6 to 10 CUC per person for a whole meal, including an alcoholic beverage. Dessert is also included and usually consists of a delicious, chocolate ice cream blended with coconut flakes, served in a frozen coconut shell. In keeping with the French theme, an automatic 10% gratuity is added to the bill. This is rare in Havana, but is standard practice in France. The service at this restaurant is extremely courteous and far above average. Furthermore, the restaurant is located inside a large, colonial mansion which has been completely restored, so the atmosphere is very classy. On a final note, while the main restaurant occupies the first floor of the mansion, there is also another section of the restaurant located on the rooftop terrace. This area is slightly less upscale but has the advantage of being airy and fresh, even on the hottest Havana nights.

<u>PioPio (23 at the corner of 12)</u>

This is not exactly a restaurant, but rather a large, open air, state-run cafeteria. It is located just across the street from the aforementioned Cinecittà restaurant. The cafeteria is large and clean and there are seats all around the counter. The cafeteria operates 24 hours a day and is extremely popular with locals, especially the after party crowd. Meals are cheap and everything is priced in Moneda Nacional. Dishes are served with either pork or chicken, surrounded by Cuban fried rice, a cucumber salad and a portion of *vianda*. Most meals cost only 25 pesos. Drinks are sold separately, at state prices. In addition to the usual brands of beer, this cafeteria also sells some brands bottled by provincial brewers, sold under the names *Tinima* and *Bruja*. Foreigners rarely get the opportunity to try these beers, so if you are in this location, I suggest you at least have a taste. They only cost 10 pesos per bottle. Being a cafeteria, you can also buy a wide variety of other goods at this location, such as bottles of rum, tobacco products, matches and candies.

Artechef (Calle 3 at the corner of A)

This state-run restaurant is located just a few blocks away from the Malecon and both the Melia Cohiba and the Riviera hotels. In my opinion, it is one of Havana's best-kept secrets. This establishment looks very upscale, with a formally dressed staff and elegantly set tables, but the prices, in relation to the quality of food you will receive, are rock bottom. Daily specials are advertised in the window and prices range from 3 to 4 CUC per meal. Everything is priced in CUC. Unlike most of the other restaurants in this list, the table d'hôte meals here do not include an alcoholic beverage, but rather a freshly squeezed juice. The thing that really separates this restaurant from all the others is that, in addition to being a restaurant, it is also a culinary school. The school teaches modern cooking practices and allows the students a degree of artistic freedom when preparing the plates. The meats are cut, prepared and presented differently from most other restaurants in Cuba. Dishes arrive at your table looking like they are ready for a magazine cover photo. Meals are properly seasoned, have rich sauces, and food portions are satisfying without being overwhelming. In all my trips to Cuba, this is the best location I have found to get modern, high end, Cuban food at a very reasonable price.

La Kasalta (Corner of Calle 2 and Ave 5ta, in Miramar)

This large, state-run restaurant is located in Miramar, just after the Calzada Tunnel leading out of Vedado. It faces the tunnel, so it is extremely easy to find. If you want a break from Havana, venture out to Miramar, sit down at the Kasalta and enjoy a great meal. The restaurant has a sports bar theme and the food is fantastic.

Everything is priced in CUC. Most of the *ofertas* are priced at about 4 to 5 CUC and they include desert and a beer. Meal portions are generous; it will be a challenge to finish all the food. Service is fast and friendly and the ambiance is casual. In the late evening, the restaurant takes on a bar atmosphere and is a great place to have a drink and watch sports on one of their many large televisions.

Coppelia (Corner 23 and L)

It's not exactly a restaurant, but it's a great place to get a wonderful ice cream dessert after dinner, or for a snack, anytime. Coppelia is Havana's world famous ice cream parlor, serving some of the best and cheapest ice cream in Cuba. The parlor occupies a whole city block and there are usually 4 or 5 separate lines formed around the perimeter. Once you get past those exterior lines, you will have to wait a bit longer in lines located inside the building. Don't let the long wait scare you; it's well worth it. The ice cream is cold and creamy, and scoops are priced at only 1 peso (MN) each. They are served on large ice cream platters, in portions of 5 scoops each, called *ensaladas* (salads). Ask the server which flavors they are serving that day, and then place your order. It's usually best to order everything you expect to eat at one time. The servers like to turn over the tables as fast as possible, so they might not come back again to take a second order. My suggestion: order two mixed ice cream *ensaladas*, that's 10 scoops. It will be more than enough for one person. A few different pastries and cakes are also usually available, priced at 5 pesos (MN) each. Note: If you want to skip the long lines, you can choose to sit in a special "foreigners" section. Although this will be faster, you will have to pay 1 CUC per scoop, rather than the usual 1 peso (MN) per scoop. **It is perfectly legal for a foreigner to wait in the standard Cuban line and to purchase ice cream for 1 peso (MN).** Anybody who tries to convince you otherwise and to bring you to the higher priced lineup is running a scam and will likely collect a commission if you believe them. It's a common trick that jineteros play on unsuspecting foreigners. Even the ice cream parlor servers sometimes try to convince tourists to change lines. Do not believe them. Stand your ground and pay in Moneda Nacional.

Independent Paladares

As mentioned before, I don't usually recommend going to sit-down paladares because the prices tend to be more expensive than state restaurants while the food is usually the same. That being said, there are some locations which stand out, and are not overly expensive. I am sure you will be able to find a lot more throughout Havana. I will mention a few, to give you an idea of what to expect at independent locations.

Cafe Presidente Paladar (G (Los Presidentes), at the corner of 25th, Vedado)

The decor and general ambiance of this privately owned cafe/restaurant/bar is decidedly modern and upscale. It was met with some skepticism when it first opened in 2014, because locals assumed the prices were very high, so they were reluctant to even enter. But slowly, a great reputation formed. While the prices are considerably higher than average, the food quality, presentation and service is also superior. Domestic beers cost 2 CUC. Popular mixed drinks and cocktails are in the 2 CUC to 4 CUC range. Pizzas, pasta, hamburgers and sandwiches are in the 4 CUC to 6 CUC range. The restaurant is non smoking and fully air conditioned.

El Balcon (28 between 31 and 33, (just west of the intersection of Zapata and 26)

This is a formal, sit down restaurant located in the Nuevo Vedado neighborhood. There is an interior, air conditioned area, as well as a large exterior terrace, which overlooks the western part of the city and offers gorgeous sunset views. Prices are in CUC and most main dishes are priced in the 5 to 6 CUC range. These do not include dessert or drinks. This restaurant usually has *oferta* specials which cost 7 CUC. These will include generous main dishes of shrimp or pork fillets, as well as sides of tamales, rice, beans and *vianda*. Dessert and a mojito or juice are also included. The ambiance in this restaurant, and especially on the terrace, is very relaxing, and it is a great place to have a fancy meal at an independent location, without breaking the bank.

La Catedral (Calle 8 #106, between Calzada and 5th, Vedado, Tel 830 0793)

La Catedral opened its doors in 2013 and was an instant hit. Almost overnight it became one of the most popular independent restaurant / bars in Vedado. And there is good reason for that. The restaurant has an old world decor with a Spanish hacienda theme. You can see the owners spent a lot of money on decor, creating a relaxing and intimate atmosphere. More importantly, the food is fantastic, and affordable. The menu is quite large, and although some seafood specialties can get a bit pricy (in the 10 CUC+ range), most of the main dishes are priced at around 5 CUC or less. Service is speedy and friendly, as should be expected from an independent restaurant, and an automatic 10% gratuity is added to all meals. In the late evening, this restaurant takes on more of a bar feel, serving a wide assortment of moderately priced drinks. For either lunch or supper, it is highly suggested to make reservations ahead of time, as there is often a healthy lineup of patrons outside. Hours of operation noon to midnight.

Pizzas Pachy (17, between 10 and 12)

This used to be a simple street-side food stand selling pizzas and spaghetti. Over the years it has leveraged its reputation for great food into a full-scale restaurant. The street-side stand still operates, pumping out delicious and cheap pizzas (10 pesos each) to the masses, but for those desiring a more formal, air conditioned setting, the restaurant at the end of the driveway is there to meet your needs. The restaurant is small, but the portions are large and the food is tasty. Food is priced in Moneda Nacional, while drinks are priced in CUC. Pizzas, spaghetti and lasagna are priced at about 50 to 60 pesos and are served with Pachy's signature spicy, oily tomato sauce. Drinks cost 1 to 2 CUC each. Pachy's is very popular with the local crowd and considered by some to have one of the best pizzas in Havana. Orders at the street side stand are much cheaper and, while portions are smaller, the food is equally delicious.

Pachy's was also one of the first pizzerias in Cuba to offer home delivery service. You can call in your pizza order by dialing their phone number (53 7 833 8417) and your order will be delivered directly to your door. Large, family size pizzas (equivalent to a medium sized North American pizza) will cost about 3 CUC to 4 CUC depending on which toppings you choose. It is customary to give the delivery driver a small tip.

<u>La Favorita (510 J Street, between 23 and 25)</u>

This small paladar offers cheap, authentic Cuban cuisine in a lively outdoor atmosphere. It's an open air restaurant located just beside a delightful park, near the corner of 23 and J. Signs at the counter prominently display the menu as well as the specials of the day. Prices are indicated in Moneda Nacional but can also be paid in CUC. Most oferta meals cost between 25 and 35 pesos (MN). This restaurant is very popular with university students and people who work in the nearby hospital centers. The establishment is family-run and the service is impeccable. The atmosphere is relaxed and welcoming. The owner is always present to make sure that everything is to your satisfaction.

The Wonderful Beaches in Havana

Almost everybody knows about the beautiful beaches in Cuba but most people are not aware that there are fantastic beaches very close to Havana. These are located about 30 kilometers east of Old Havana and are named the *Playas del Este*, which literally means "eastern beaches." The *Playas del Este* area is made up of several separate beaches, the most popular of which are Playa Santa Maria, Boca Ciega and Guanabo.

The beaches are typically wide, with soft white sand. The ocean water is gentle and usually shallow even 100 meters from the shore. At these beaches, tourists are few and far between, mostly because there are not many hotels in the area. Furthermore, it can be expensive (20 CUC or more) to get to the beach from Havana, unless you know how to use the communal taxi routes.

Cubans love to go to the beach in the months of May through September, and particularly in the hot summer months of July and August. On summer weekends, tens of thousands of locals flock to the *Playas del Este*. In the months of December and January, these beaches are almost completely deserted. Despite the climate being warm year round, most Cubans find that the temperatures in the winter months, which, on a cool day, *only* hover around 25 degree Celsius, are just too cold for beach-going. Personally, I consider the *Playas del Este* a great place to visit, any time of the year. And once you know how to get there in a taxi particular, you will surely consider them one of the cheapest, and most fun destinations in the Havana area.

Getting to the Beach in a Taxi Particular

The main route for all the taxis particulares going from Havana to the *Playas del Este* starts at an unmarked taxi depot in Old Havana, located at the corner of Agramonte and Mision streets. This is the only location where you will be able to find a taxi particular which will take you to the beach. The main taxi route runs from Old Havana until the large beach town of Guanabo, located 30 km east. The taxi particular fare to get there is only 50 peso (MN). I will give you step by step instructions on exactly how to find the taxi depot and how to get to the beach.

Finding the Taxi Depot (corner of Agramonte and Mision)

1) **Get to the Capitolio**.

2) **Orient yourself in front of the main entrance of the building** (where the steps are). The main entrance of the Capitolio faces east. The street directly in front of the building is called Prado. Directly in front of the Capitol building is the intersection of the streets Prado and Brasil (Teniente Rey)

3) **Walk across Prado street and continue walking east along Brasil, for just one block**, until you reach Agramonte Street. Agramonte runs parallel to Prado.

4) **Turn right on Agramonte** (direction south), and walk for 6 blocks (should take you about 10 minutes)

5) **The main taxi depot is located at the corner of Agramonte and Mision Street.**

Taking the Taxi

Once you get to the taxi area, you will see at least a half dozen taxis particulares. There will likely be a lot of people in the area too, waiting to get into taxis. There will be at least a few men shouting, "*Guanabo, Guanabo.*" These men are the taxi organizers and are alerting passengers that the taxis will be traveling all the way to the eastern suburb of Guanabo. This is where you want to go. Approach one of these organizers, tell them you want to go to Guanabo, and they will place you into one of the waiting taxis. Never pay anything to these men. You only pay the taxi driver at the end of the trip.

Most of the taxis particulares going to the *Playas del Este* are station wagons with an extra row of seats, making them capable of holding up to nine passengers. The cars almost always travel fully occupied, so as to make the trip financially viable for the driver. The ride usually takes about 30 minutes and, as mentioned before, costs 50 pesos (MN) per person.

Where to Get Off

Although these taxis will take you all the way from Old Havana to the town of Guanabo, you can get off at any point along the route. One of the closest beaches is named Bacuranao. It is very small and

170

not so popular. Further east, there are a few tourist hotels (Atlantico and Tropicoco) located near the town of Santa Maria del Mar. The beach here is great, but the area is isolated, so your options for drinking, dining and entertainment are very limited.

I recommend riding the taxi a few kilometers further, into the town of Guanabo. The beach in this area is one of the best and, most importantly, Guanabo is filled with restaurants, stores, discos and casas particulares. It is far and away the most popular beach of the *Playas del Este*. When Havana residents talks about going to the beach, this is the place they are referring to.

The taxis will always drive along Guanabo's main street (Ave. 5ta), which runs parallel to the beach. I suggest getting off just when you start to see the action, shortly after the roundabout in the road. The beach is particularly nice in this area and you can always explore the rest of the town on foot. If you are unsure of where to get out, just tell the taxi driver that you want to go to the *Playa de Guanabo* (Guanabo Beach) and he will let you off in the right spot.

Getting Back To Havana

Since Guanabo is the most popular beach in *Playas del Este*, there will always be many taxis particulares to take you back to Havana. After your day of swimming and sunbathing, just go back to the main street (Ave. 5ta), where you were initially dropped off, and hail a taxi particular traveling west (driving on the beach-side lane). Tell the driver you are heading to *La Habana*. Most of the taxis driving west will be going to Havana, so it will be very easy to find a ride. The trip costs 50 pesos (MN).

Important Note: If you are leaving the beach late at night (after 10pm) it can be more difficult to find a taxi particular going to Havana. In peak beach season, it's usually not a problem, but in the low season, it can sometimes take a few tries before you snag a ride. In the worst case scenario, you might have to pay the driver a bit extra (a few CUC) to sway his decision in your favor.

<u>Other Options to Get to the Beach</u>

There are several other ways to get to Guanabo and the Playas del Este beaches. Honestly, I don't recommend any of them. A state-run taxi will be an expensive option, costing you a minimum of 20 CUC to get you to the beach, plus another 20 CUC for the return trip. There is a city bus (#400) that can take you from Havana to Guanabo for only one peso, but it passes only once per hour, and it can be extremely overcrowded, with massive lineups to board. Finally, there are large, private buses which charge only 5 to 10 pesos (MN) to reach Guanabo. Most of these buses only operate in the peak season and are often ridiculously overcrowded. Moreover, you must ride the bus all the way to Guanabo, without any option of stopping at another beach along the way.

Riding the Hershey Train

Cuba used to have one of the most well developed railway networks in Latin America. By most accounts, the system is currently dilapidated, due to old infrastructure and decades of neglect. Many of the trains still run, but delays and breakdowns are frequent. As a mode of transportation, the rail option is rather poor. But in terms of nostalgia and fun, it can be quite the trip.

Although there are several train routes in Cuba, I will only give you a quick breakdown of the one located closest to Havana. This is the most popular one used by foreigners, although most of the travelers are Cuban. The Hershey train is an electric rail-car which departs 3 times per day from the Casablanca station, on the eastern shore of the Havana harbor, and travels all the way to the city of Matanzas, located about 100 km east of Havana. In between, the train makes dozens of short stops and, in many cases, will let you off on demand, anywhere along the route, if conditions permit.

The Casablanca station is located outside of the city of Havana, on the other side of the Bay of Havana. You can get to the station by taxi, but the cheapest and shortest option is to take the Casablanca ferry. This is a ferry which departs from the Havana ferry terminal (as mentioned in the Havana Suburbs section (p.127)) located at the corner of San Pedro and Santa Clara in Old Havana. When you arrive at the ferry station, make sure to inquire if the next ferry is traveling to Regla or Casablanca. You want to get on the one going to Casablanca. The ferry ride only costs 0.2 pesos (MN). Most foreigners don't have change this small, and simply pay 1 peso (MN).

Once you are at the Casablanca landing, you will see the Casablanca train terminal just to the north. It's a very small terminal, looking more like a tram stop. The overhead electric wires will indicate exactly where it is.

The price to use the train depends on how far you want to go. The main stop between Havana and Matanzas is located in the miniscule town of Hershey (renamed to Camilo Cienfuegos). It is at the halfway point between the two cities. Travel up to this stop costs 1.40 CUC for foreigners. Travel all the way to Matanzas costs a total of 2.80 CUC. Most foreigners who simply want to take the train for the nostalgic experience will simply take the first leg of the trip, getting off at the town of Hershey for a quick exploration, and to wait for the return train to bring them back to Havana. It's important to note that about 1 km north of the town of Hershey, there is the larger, coastal town of Santa Cruz del Norte. It's easy to walk to and interesting to explore, and you are almost sure to be the only foreigner there.

In order to get back to Havana, simply go back to the station, pay the fare, and take the next train.

The train schedule is listed below, but note that it can change without notice, mostly due to equipment failures. On some days, when there are electrical problems, the train doesn't operate at all.

Schedule:

Havana to Matanzas

Departure	Havana >	Hershey >	Matanzas >
1 -->	4:45am	6:15am	8:10am
2 -->	12:20pm	1:55pm	3:40pm
3 -->	4:35pm	6:10pm	8pm

Matanzas to Havana

Departure	Matanzas >	Hershey >	Havana >
1 -->	4:35am	6:25am	8:00am
2 -->	12:10pm	1:55pm	3:30pm
3 -->	4:25pm	6:10pm	7:40pm

Special Note: Some guides mention that the Hershey Train is an excellent way to get from Havana to the Playas del Este. This is misleading. If you simply want to experience a train ride in Cuba, this can be a fun outing, but if your intentions are to go to the beach easily and cheaply, this will not be the best choice of route. As mentioned, a taxi particular will take you from Havana to Guanabo beach in about 30 minutes and cost you 50 pesos (MN) (about 2 CUC). The Hershey train will cost you slightly less (0.75 CUC), but you will have to take a ferry to Casablanca, and then take the train, and hope that both of these services are operational. Forgetting about all the other common delays, the train ride from Havana to Guanabo usually takes over 45 minutes, and the actual train stop is located in an empty field, several kilometers outside of Guanabo. It can easily take you an additional hour to walk all the way to the beach. If you want an adventure, it can be a fun trip. If you just want to get to the beach, it's a hassle, and it can take more than 2 hours, on a good day.

Havana Carnival

Shhh, don't tell anyone, but the carnival scene in Cuba is absolutely wild! Although definitely not as famous as the ones in Rio de Janeiro, New Orleans or throughout Europe, the carnivals in Cuba are among some of the most entertaining events in the country. There are two main carnivals in Cuba. One is hosted in Havana and the other in Santiago de Cuba. If you get a chance, you should definitely check out both. While the carnival in Santiago is usually slightly larger, there has been a great effort in the last few years to expand the size and entertainment quality at the Havana carnival. At this rate, in a few more years, it could grow into one of the largest and most popular in the world.

And the best thing about the Havana carnival is that very few tourists go to it. The carnival is usually hosted in mid-August (dates change yearly), which is the low period in the tourist season and a time when many Cubans take their summer vacations. This creates the perfect environment for a massive, city-wide party, attended almost exclusively by locals. During carnival week there are hundreds of parties, parades and festivals on streets and in parks around the city. But the main stage is set along the Malecon, particularly near the intersection of 23. This area is completely closed to vehicle traffic and, at night, tens of thousands of locals crowd into the street. Hundreds of food stands pop up, selling low-priced meals and there are dozens of state-operated beer and alcohol stands. Beers usually cost only a few pesos (MN). The atmosphere can get chaotic at times, but once the music starts and the scantily clad dancers get on stage, the tone is set for one of the most energetic shows you will ever see. Best of all, the entertainment is all completely free.

As mentioned before, dates for the Havana Carnival change yearly, so if you are planning to go, make sure to check the schedule online before reserving your trip. And be warned, it gets really hot in Havana in August, even at night, and especially on a street packed with a hundred thousand revelers. But don't let that dissuade you, carnival is great fun and, at least for now, it seems to be one of Havana's little-known entertainment secrets.

Havana's Chinatown

Havana's *Barrio Chino* (Chinatown) is one of the oldest in Latin America. Chinese immigration to Cuba started in the mid 19th century, when Cantonese workers were brought to Cuba to work on the sugar cane plantations, and continued up into the early 20th century. Many of these Chinese workers eventually settled in Havana, but after the Cuban Revolution, there was a rather large Chinese exodus from the island.

Presently, the Chinese population in Havana is very low and the *Barrio Chino* consists of little more than a few small streets where half a dozen Chinese themed restaurants have clustered. Officially, the *barrio* starts at the corner of Ave. de Italia and Zanja, where a small park has a memorial to Chinese immigrants. One block further west, near the corner of Zanja and Rayo, you will see an archway that extends over a tight, pedestrian-only street named Cuchillo. This is the main center of the *Barrio Chino*. There are a few Chinese-themed restaurants. Most of the food at these establishments is standard Cuban fare with a slight Chinese twist. Most of the patrons are tourists. The prices are on the expensive side (10 CUC or more per person).

While Havana's Chinatown may be a disappointment, I still suggest coming to the area and exploring some of the other shops and restaurants in the neighborhood. As mentioned in the Shopping (p.144) section of this guide, there are several large retail centers on Ave. de Italia, near Chinatown, as well as a few markets and artisanal bazaars. Furthermore, perhaps spurred by the influx of tourists coming to the area, there are quite a few new Cuban restaurants, bars and independent food stands in operation along this part of Zanja Street. At night especially, this area becomes crowded with locals, eating, drinking and enjoying their evening.

Havana Entertainment Options

Havana is a city that lives and breathes excitement. It radiates a vibrant culture like no other city in the world. There are thousands of great places to visit and explore, day and night, and most of them are extremely inexpensive, or free. While the following list is not exhaustive, it will give you a good idea of what to expect and perhaps a few ideas on how you can discover other interesting entertainment options on your own. The best thing to remember is that half the fun in any adventure comes from the searching. So as long as you are out and about, walking the Havana streets and interacting with locals, it is impossible to get bored.

Free Fun

Explore a Beautiful Old Building

Havana has a wealth of majestic, old buildings. While many of these are crumbling and in desperate need of repair, most are also architectural marvels and shockingly beautiful. The neighborhoods of Vedado and Central Havana are packed with gorgeous apartment buildings, with some being well over 100 years old. You can freely walk into most of these buildings and explore the lobbies, hallways, and all other public areas. If you're lucky, a resident might even invite you inside their apartment for a cup of coffee and a chat.

One of my favorite buildings to visit is located at the corner of 25 and G, in Vedado. The huge, red bricked apartment complex has amazing architecture and clearly stands apart from all other buildings in the area. You can simply walk inside and take the elevator to the 9th or 10th floor. There, you will see a lookout offering incredible, unobstructed views of the whole city.

Explore a Dilapidated Building

Some apartment buildings in Havana are beyond repair. They have crumbled to pieces after years of neglect. Despite this, a fair number are still inhabited by people, although living conditions are very poor. If you want to see the harsh reality for yourself, you can enter some of the dilapidated buildings in Central Havana, especially those near the Capitolio. The front doors are usually left open and a long, steep, flight of stairs leads up from the street. You can just walk in and explore the various levels. Buildings like these can house dozens of families per level and, in all likelihood, nobody will even notice you roaming the hallways. As with most things in Cuba, the only private areas are those closed off by a locked door. Everything else is public.

Explore a Fancy Hotel

Just because you are not paying the expensive fare to stay at a fancy hotel, doesn't mean you can't freely enter, explore, and use some of the facilities.

The Hotel Nacional (entrance on 21 and O, Vedado) is a prime example. Just walk through the hotel's main lobby to the rear doors which open up to an immense outdoor seating area overlooking the Malecon. There is a stage as well as a bar which serves relatively inexpensive drinks. It is always free to visit this area, and you can relax for hours, even if you don't order any drinks at all. There's even a little museum with antique cannons.

The Habana Libre Hotel (Corner 23 and L) is another great example of a place you can explore for free. While the main lobby is usually crowded with tourists, the mezzanine level is almost always deserted. Just walk up the majestic wooden staircase. The atrium is filled with natural light and surrounded by lounge chairs that you can use any time of the day. Furthermore, it is completely air conditioned and there is WIFI coverage (pay per use). There are also hundreds of photos on the walls, chronicling the time when Fidel Castro occupied the hotel after the Cuban Revolution.

For a bit more excitement, you can take the elevator up to the 25th floor and enter the *El Turquino* disco. Although the disco only officially opens at night, the entrance doors are usually unlocked during the day and you are free to enter. Sometimes there are a few workers in the disco, cleaning or setting up decorations; they will not mind your presence at all. The disco has wrap-around windows offering a panoramic view of the whole city. Just take a seat and marvel at the sights.

<u>Check Out a Park</u>

There are dozens of great parks scattered around Havana. Most of them offer comfortable benches and a good deal of shade. Many have large public monuments or statues dedicated to war heroes and revolutionary leaders. There are also some nature reserves which offer a chance to see lush, virgin vegetation in a calm surrounding.

Parque John Lennon (corner 17 and 6) is a famous park, popular with locals and tourists alike. The park gets its name from the large, bronze statue of John Lennon, seated on one of the park benches. Right beside the park is the Centro Cultural Submarino Amarillo, a Beatles themed lounge bar where Beatles cover bands play live music almost nightly.

Parque Almendares (also called *Gran Parque Metropolitano* or *Isla Josefina*) is Havana's largest nature park. It's located just past the Calle 23 bridge (*Puente Almendares*), that leads into the Playa neighborhood. In total, the park covers over 300 hectares of land. The park borders the *Almendares* river and has a forest with lush vegetation. There are footpaths crossing through the park and a small road runs along the perimeter. A large children's playground is located at the entrance to the park, almost directly under the *Puente Almendares.*

179

Quinta de los Molinos (just west of the corner of Salvador Allende and Infanta) is a large Spanish estate, surrounded by lush gardens and tranquil ponds. After years of renovations, it was recently opened to the public. It was once the site of the Havana Botanical Gardens, and the whole area still has the general feel of a large garden. All the plants and trees are labeled and categorized and the grounds are tirelessly manicured. The Maximo Gomez museum is also located on the same campus. It is free to enter the park and explore the grounds. Entrance into the estate and museum costs extra. Note: There have been rumors that the park may be converted into a horticultural research center in the near future and closed to the public.

Parque Lenin is one of the largest city parks in the Americas. It's a sprawling nature reserve, covering almost 670 hectares, flanked by both the Cuban National Zoo and the National Botanical Garden. The park is noted for its two large lakes, wildlife exhibits of crocodiles and fish, and for the massive statue of Vladimir Lenin.

Although some areas of the park look dated, it is currently undergoing a major facelift and is still considered one of the premier recreational areas in Havana. It is located off the *Calzada de Bejucal* road, in the Arroyo Naranjo neighborhood, 20 km south of Central Havana. Entrance is free.

Visit Hotel Conde de Villanueva (202 Calle Mercaderes, near the corner of Lamparilla, Old Havana)

The Hotel Conde de Villanueva was once a huge colonial mansion, with a rich history dating back to 1714. It has recently been restored and converted into a boutique hotel with 9 rooms. There is also a bar, tobacco shop and restaurant on the premises. It is completely free to enter the building and walk around. The front doors open to a palatial inner courtyard, filled with sunlight and surrounded by columns and stained glass windows. The atmosphere is peaceful and relaxed. There are usually a couple of friendly peacock birds wandering around the courtyard. There are seats and tables where you can sit down. On the second level there is cigar shop, smoking lounge and bar. During the day, in the cigar shop, you will usually find a man, seated, rolling cigars. It's an interesting process to watch, especially if you have never seen it. The bar is air conditioned, eclectically decorated and has many comfortable leather chairs. The bar and cigar shop are not well advertised and, as such, they are usually completely empty of patrons. But don't be shy to walk in, look around and make yourself at home.

People-Watching

Go for an evening walk through Central Havana. While this neighborhood is crowded and smoggy during the day, it really relaxes at night. It's common to see children playing in the streets and young people hanging out on doorsteps, chatting and singing late into the evening. Old men smoke cigars and chat on street corners while the younger ones set up square tables, under streetlamps, and play dominoes until well past midnight.

A Day on the Malecon

Relax on the Malecon during the day. You will see a side of Havana that most foreigners miss as they hustle from one tourist attraction to the next. On hot days, young kids swim and play in the water just off the Malecon. On mornings, when the water is calm, fishermen congregate along the Malecon, particularly in the area west of Paseo, casting their lines far into the ocean. Divers also sometimes snorkel along the reef, in their search for octopus and other sea creatures. At various times throughout the year, the Malecon is also the site of fashion shows, concerts and art exhibits. These usually take place along the section of the Malecon located near Central Havana.

The Malecon at Night

As discussed before, the Malecon is a fantastic place to visit at any time of the day. It is particularly active on weekend nights when the weather is hot. Faced with sweltering temperatures inside their homes, Havana locals flock to the Malecon where they can relax in the cool ocean breeze or party with their friends as they share a bottle of rum. The Malecon is most active where it intersects with La Rampa (23). On occasion the lower portion of Calle 23 is closed off to car traffic due to the crowd sizes. Thursday, Friday, Saturday and Sunday nights, this is the place to be.

Outdoor Dance Party

Every Sunday afternoon, there is a large, free, outdoor dance party along Calle Hamel in Central Havana (just south of the corner of San Lazaro and Calle Hospital). Along this street there are also many artistic murals and vendors selling souvenirs and handcrafted art.

If you are looking for a less touristy atmosphere, you can visit the *Gran Palenque* esplanade (Calle 4, between 5 and Calzada, Nuevo Vedado) for the *Sábado de La Rumba* dance festivities, held every Saturday from 3pm to 6pm. The music plays loud and fast. Surrounded by excited locals and a catchy beat, even the stiffest dancers are guaranteed to find their rhythm.

G Street at Night

If you're searching for something a little less raucous, you can always head over to Calle G on a weekend night. Despite the crowds of people gathered along the wide median running the length of this street, the atmosphere is decidedly more sophisticated than on the Malecon. Most of the revelers are university students or artists who live in the Vedado neighborhood. The largest crowds gather close to the corner of 23. There is a cheap, open air bar as well as several cafes, restaurants and state-run cafeterias which ensure everybody has enough to eat and drink.

Get Lost

The most interesting parts of Havana are well off the beaten path. Break free from the tourist hot spots and take a break from the relatively upscale downtown Vedado area. Walking or taking a short taxi ride to any corner of Havana that you haven't visited yet, putting your map away and letting your curiosity be your guide is bound to be an enlightening experience. And it's comforting to know that you will always feel perfectly safe and welcome, no matter how run-down the neighborhood may appear. There are many areas in and around Havana that tourists rarely venture to but where there is much to see and experience.

In Vedado, one of the least gentrified areas is located north of Linea street, between N and A. In Central Havana, almost the whole neighborhood is considered underprivileged, especially the southern sections, stretching into the large El Cerro neighborhood. Further east, the hilly neighborhood of San Miguel del Padron is always interesting and completely unexplored by tourists. West of Havana, the suburbs of Marianao and La Lisa make for an interesting day trip and are relatively easy to get to by communal taxi, as explained in the <u>Havana Suburbs</u> section (p.127).

<u>Amateur Sports</u>

It's no secret that sports are very popular in Cuba. Amateur teams playing soccer (futbol or pelota) or baseball (béisbol) are always playing in parks and empty fields. If you're the athletic type, you are certainly welcome to join in the game. Just stand around the sidelines for a minute and you will soon be invited to participate. If watching is more your thing, there are some really great locations in Havana to view amateurs play in organized teams. Best of all, watching these games is completely free.

Estadio Universitario Juan Abrantes - Located near the corner of 27 de Noviembre and Calle J, in Vedado, just behind the main University of Havana campus, this large stadium hosts minor league sporting events almost every evening. During the day you can watch practices and pick-up games. It's usually free to enter. If a popular team is playing it might cost a few pesos (MN) for a seat.

Estadio Jose Marti - Located at the corner of G and the Malecon, you can always find an amateur team kicking a soccer ball around at this large, soviet-style stadium. The facility has certainly seen better days, but it's a nice reminder that it doesn't take much to have fun in Havana.

El Hueco - Located just a few blocks east of Estadio Jose Marti, at the corner of Calzada and J, is a huge, grassy field which the locals call *El Hueco* (the gap). While mostly deserted during the day, at night this field transforms into an amateur sports mecca. It's not uncommon to see an organized baseball game *and* a soccer game taking place on the lower field, as well as a basketball game happening in the upper area, where a crumbling court is located. Locals watch from makeshift bleachers. Vendors, with pushcarts full of treats, swarm this area on hot evenings, while the state store, located at the corner of the lot, makes sure that there is enough beer and rum for everybody.

Centro Juvenil J.A. Echevarría - Formerly the Havana Tennis Club, this complex, located at the corner of Calzada and 12th street, has a large baseball field in the back, overlooking the Malecon. It's very common to see pick-up games played there during the day, while organized teams take over on evenings and weekends. Entrance is usually free. You can also just sit on the Malecon and watch the games through the fence.

The Beach

If you're looking to beat the summer heat, your best option is to head on over to the beach. I have explained precisely how to use communal taxis to get to the beautiful Playas del Este, in the section titled Getting to the Beach In a Taxi Particular (p.169). If you are just looking to take a dip in the ocean and don't really care for traveling outside the city, you can always visit one of the many mini-beaches that line the shore in the Miramar neighborhood. These beaches are rather rustic; most of them have no sand at all. They arc mostly just rocky paths leading to the ocean. But for a quick dip, on a hot day, that's all you need. If you are more adventurous, you can also just swim off the Malecon. It's a rocky area, so you have to be careful, but if you find a spot where other locals are doing it, stick with them and you should be fine.

Low-Priced Places to Visit

While you can definitely have a fun time in Havana for free, there are also several great locations to explore, which, despite costing a bit of money, are still very economical. As mentioned before, Havana is generally a very inexpensive city, especially if you stay away from the most touristy areas. That being said, for a few of the locations listed below, there are two tier pricing options: one price for locals, and another price for foreigners. In most cases the foreigner price is still a great bargain. Nevertheless, I suggest always trying your best to pay the Cuban price. A simple trick is to ask a local to buy you an entrance ticket and offer to pay for their ticket as well. Instead of paying 5 CUC you can pay just a few pesos (MN) and pretend you are a local.

Ferry to Regla or Casablanca

As mentioned in the Havana Suburbs (p.127) section, taking the ferry to the town of Regla, located just on the other side of the Bay of Havana, is always a fun expedition, and the price is only 0.2 pesos (MN). The ferry terminal is located in Old Havana, at the corner of San Pedro and Santa Clara streets. There are actually two ferry routes operating from this terminal. While the Regla line is the most popular, you can also take the ferry to the Casablanca terminal, also located on the other side of the Bay. At this terminal you will find the Hershey Train Station.

Ride the Hershey Electric Train

For those travelers who want to break free from Havana for a while and enjoy the view of the Cuban countryside, a short ride on the antique Hershey Electric Train is a perfect option. The train departs 3 times per day and can take you as far as the city of Matanzas. For a shorter trip, I recommend simply getting off in the small eastern town of Santa Cruz del Nord. It's about an hour and a half from Havana, and the train fare will only cost you 1.40 CUC. Refer to the section on <u>Riding the Hershey Train</u> (p.172) for more details.

<u>Camera Obscura Show (Corner Muralla and San Ignacio, overlooking the Plaza Vieja in Old Havana)</u>

Right at the corner of Muralla and San Ignacio you will see a large sign advertising the camera obscura. The camera obscura is an optical device, placed on a tower, atop the building, which uses a mirror and pulleys to display a 360 degree image of Havana. The small audience enters a dimly lit room and stands around a large, circular viewing dish. The operator of the device gives a comical presentation, in English and Spanish, and zooms in on interesting things that are happening, in real time, in the city. The show last less than 10 minutes, but it is entertaining and only costs 2 CUC for foreigners. Camera obscura devices used to be very popular throughout the world, but there are currently fewer than 70 still in operation today. After the show, you can walk onto the rooftop observation deck that overlooks the Plaza Vieja and offers great views of Old Havana. Hours of operation are Tuesday to Saturday from 9am to 5pm. Sunday from 9am to 1pm. It is usually closed on Monday.

<u>Christopher Columbus Cemetery</u>

The massive *Cementerio de Cristóbal Colón,* located at the corner of Zapata and 12th Street, is truly a sight to see. It sprawls over 57 hectares and is covered with thousands of elaborately sculpted memorials. It is considered to be one of the greatest historical cemeteries in the world. Entrance for locals is free, but for foreigners there is a 5 CUC admittance charge. However, there is rarely a guard at the main doors so you can usually enter for free. Just walk right in.

Hotel Pools

For a small fee, most hotels in Havana will allow foreigners and locals to use their pool facilities. The prices for admittance change frequently so it is best to confirm before planning your day. Fees range from as low as 5 CUC at hotels located in the suburbs, like the Hotel Neptuno-Triton (3ra and 74 in Miramar), to up to 25 CUC at fancier hotels such as the Hotel Nacional (Corner 21 and O). It's important to note that at most hotels you usually also receive a food and drink voucher, valued at about half of the pool admittance price. This entitles you to a few free drinks and appetizers.

Drink Guarapo Frio

A trip to Cuba would not be complete without tasting guarapo. A refreshing, sugarcane juice drink, often served with crushed ice. Here are a few popular locations to get guarapo frio in Havana.

- Simon Bolivar, right beside the Capitolio (Central Havana). This is a crowded place which is often closed on Mondays. The location is in front of one of the busiest bus stops in the city, so they charge 2 pesos per cup instead of the usual 1 peso (Moneda Nacional)
- Arsenal Street (Old Havana), in front of the train station. Probably the best Guarapo place in Havana. The juice is always icy cold. Usually there is a good lineup because of the people waiting for trains / buses.
- Neptuno Street (Central Havana). There are several places to get guaparo on Neptuno street. There are some stand alone locations as well as many small stands located in fruit markets.
- Intersection of Carlos Tercero and Infanta (Central Havana). One of the most popular locations in the neighborhood. Usually closed on Monday.
- H Street, near the corner of 25 (Vedado). Walk all the way up H street and you will find a tiny fruit market. There is a guarapo stand there, one of the only ones in Vedado.

187

This is just a very small sampling of the hundreds of guarapo stands that are located throughout Havana. By wandering around the city you can find your own favorite place.

El Morro and La Cabaña

As you explore Havana you will no doubt notice the magnificent castle and fortress, located just on the other side of the Bay of Havana. At the very tip of the mouth of the harbor there is an impressive, steep-walled castle, perched over a rocky cliff, with a tall lighthouse. This structure is called El Morro (formally named Castillo de los Tres Reyes Magos del Morro). South of El Morro there is a massive fortress, stretching almost 700 meters along the waterfront hillside. This structure is called La Cabaña (formally named Fortaleza de San Carlos de la Cabaña). The two attractions are independent and you will have to pay separate entrance fees for each.

The El Morro castle is well preserved and has a maritime museum on the ground level. The star attraction is the lighthouse, which you can walk to the top of, offering an unparalleled view of the ocean and the city of Havana. It is probably the best place in the city to view the sunset. Basic admission is 6 CUC. A visit to the top of the lighthouse costs an additional 2 CUC.

A ten minute walk south of El Morro, you will find La Cabaña. It is the largest Spanish colonial fortress in the Americas. It has been completely restored and hosts a Che Guevara and military museum. There are also bars, restaurants, souvenir stalls and a cigar shop. The highlight of La Cabaña is the nightly medieval re-enactment of the closing of the city gates and harbor, along with the firing of a cannon at exactly 9PM. On most nights, the sound of the cannon firing can be heard throughout Havana. Coming to this fortress, especially in the evenings, is a very popular activity for locals and it tend to get very crowded, so it is recommended to plan ahead and arrive a bit early. The show starts each night at 8pm. The price for foreigners to visit the nighttime show is 6 CUC for basic admission and 8 CUC if you want a balcony seat.

Both El Morro and La Cabaña are easily accessible by taxi but you can also get to them cheaply by taking either the P5 or P11 buses which will pick you up in front of the Capitolio, on the east side of Prado street. These buses run frequently and only cost half a peso (MN) to use. Get off at the first stop, on the other side of the harbor and then either walk up the hill north (towards the ocean) for El Morro, or walk south for La Cabaña. Another option is to take the ferry from Old Havana to the Casablanca terminal, and then just walk north, up the hill beside the station (as will be discussed in the following section).

El Cristo

In Casablanca, tucked conveniently between the Hershey electric train station and the La Cabaña fortress, you will find an interesting and often overlooked attraction called El Cristo de La Habana. It is a 20 meter tall (66 feet), marble sculpture of Jesus, perched on a hilltop park. Surrounding the statue is an esplanade with seating areas, green spaces and a panoramic view of the harbor and most of the city of Havana. Other than the small cost of taking the ferry or other transportation to Casablanca, it's totally free to enter this park.

The street signs leading you to El Cristo are rather ambiguous. However, since Casablanca is such a small town, it is not difficult to locate this attraction. The road directly in front of the Casablanca ferry terminal leads up the main hill. Walk up the road, and then follow it left (north) as it gently slopes its way through a small forest, until reaching the El Cristo statue. This winding road is called Arret de los Cocos, although it is not very clearly indicated. From the ferry terminal to the statue it is about a 20 minute walk.

The Arret de los Cocos road passes along the perimeter of the La Cabaña fortress and there are various, indicated paths that you can take to enter the fortress grounds through side entrances. The road eventually passes in front of the main fortress gates (at the top of the hill) and then continues on to El Morro. Note that while the southern side of La Cabaña is located only about 5 minutes walking away from El Cristo, El Morro is a further 25 minute walk away. If you should get tired, you can always find a taxi or bicitaxi near the El Cristo to bring you.

Watch a Movie

There are a lot of movie theaters in Havana and watching movies is a very popular pastime. While these cinemas will show international and American films, there is also a well developed Cuban film industry, and homegrown movies are extremely popular. Typically, the admission to see a film is between 1 and 2 pesos (MN). Foreigners are sometimes charged in CUC. Some of the most popular cinemas in Vedado are Cinema Yara (23 and L), Riviera (23 and G), Chaplin (23, between 10 and 12) and La Rampa (23 and O).

Watch a Play or Live Show

Small theater productions are also very popular in Havana. The sets may be simply designed, but the acting is top quality. It is very common for major Cuban movie stars to perform in small, local productions. The price of admission to these shows is often minimal, usually costing no more than 5 pesos (MN). The most popular small theater in Vedado is the Bertolt Brecht Theater, located at the corner of 13 and I. Larger theaters such as the Karl Marx (Corner 1ra and 10 in Miramar) and the Teatro Nacional (Paseo and 39, facing the Plaza de la Revolución) are used to stage bigger productions and as concert venues for popular bands. The price of admission in these theaters can be much higher, depending on the show, sometimes as high as 10 CUC.

The Ballet

Cubans take the ballet very seriously. This could be due to Cuba's close ties with Russia, or the fact that dance, in any form, is highly regarded. Either way, the ballet is one of the greatest shows you can see in Havana. Performances take place on most Friday, Saturday and Sunday nights, in the amazing *Gran Teatro de La Habana* located in Old Havana (Corner of Paseo and San Rafael, beside the Capitolio). The building is an elaborate representation of neo-baroque architecture and is a wonderful sight to see on its own. Backstage tours of the building cost only 2 CUC. For the actual ballet performance, the price of admittance for foreigners is 20 CUC. This is rather expensive, considering that locals can get in for only 20 pesos (MN). This is a great example of a situation where you should get a local to buy a ticket for you, in Moneda Nacional. There are always dozens of people in front of the building, and for a small tip, they will be more than willing to buy you a show ticket.

Dance Classes

As mentioned earlier, there are some great places to dance for free on the weekends in Havana. If you are looking for a more formal setting to learn or practice your moves, you can always take a dance class. The *Casa del Tango*, located on Neptuno Street, just east of Ave. de Italia, in Centro Habana, is an excellent place to start. The teachers are professionals, having taught some of the leading dancers in Cuba. And contrary to the name, all forms of dance are taught at the school. Lessons start at 5 to 10 CUC per hour, but prices are very negotiable. It's free to enter on evenings to watch the nightly dance shows.

There are literally hundreds of other dance schools in Havana, and usually amateur and professional instructors linger around the schools offering private courses at discount prices. These can be very good deals. A few other professional dance studios which are popular with locals and foreigners are the *San Miguel Dance Academy* (San Miguel # 569, between Belascoain and Gervasio. Phone Number (537) 261 5572) and the *Fame Dance Academy* (San Lazaro # 72, between Carceles and Genios. Phone number 53 (5) 345 4922). Both are located in Central Havana.

Boxing Classes

It is a fact that Cuba has won more Olympic medals per-capita, than any other nation. The majority of those medals have been for the sport of boxing. In Havana, you can hone your boxing skills (or develop them from scratch, if you have none), with some of the best teachers in the world. One of the most famous boxing schools in the city is the *Gimnasio de Boxeo Rafael Trejo*, located at #815 Calle de Cuba, in the southern section of Old Havana. The school is basically just a shell of a building and the ring is antiquated, but the instructors are pros and are skilled at training all levels. You don't have to be a prize fighter to come here. You just have to possess a desire to learn. Classes start in the afternoon, around 4pm, and cost about 5 to 10 CUC per session for foreigners, depending on your negotiating ability. In the evening, the gym turns into a venue for amateur boxing matches.

Professional Baseball

I can think of no better way to spend an evening, than to be in a massive stadium, surrounded by up to 50 000 raucous Cubans, watching the legendary *Industriales* baseball team thump the opposition. In Cuba, baseball is not just a sport, it's an obsession. Everybody in Havana seems to be a fanatic. But you don't even have to be a fan to enjoy the incredible atmosphere of watching a live game. The games are fast paced and the players high caliber. Many of the best players are recruited to play in the United States each year. The regular baseball season runs from November to April. A shorter *Super Series* runs from May to July. In Havana, all games are played at the *Estadio Latinoamericano*, located in the El Cerro neighborhood, at the corner of Ave. 20 de Mayo and Calle Amenidad, a few blocks south of the Plaza de la Revolución. Tickets cost 3 CUC for foreigners and only 1 peso (MN) for locals. There is no assigned seating. You can check the schedule at the following link: www.baseballdecuba.com

Amusement Park

Yes, Havana has a theme park. It's located in the suburb of Miramar, at the corner of Ave. 5ta and 112. Originally named and modeled after the American park, Coney Island, it is now called *Isla de Coco*. It has a good selection of modern rides as well as some older ones that have been restored. Most of the attractions are geared towards children, but thrill seekers will enjoy the vintage roller coaster and the cosmonaut slinger. Admission to the park is only 1 peso (MN) but you have to pay to use the particular rides (prices range from 2 to 6 pesos (MN)). The majority of visitors are local Cubans. Hours of operation are noon to 8pm, Friday to Sunday.

Cuban National Circus

An even better attraction is the Cuban National Circus. It regularly visits the city and installs its giant, colorful tent on the *Isla de Coco* amusement park's grounds. Shows are held throughout the year and you can check the schedule at this link: www.CircoNacionalDeCuba.cu

The Aquarium

The *Acuario Nacional* is located at the corner of Ave. 3ra and Calle 62 in the Miramar. It's a large aquarium complex, bordering the ocean, where you can see all forms of marine life. The main attraction is the lively dolphin show which offers visitors the opportunity to interact with and touch the dolphins after the performance. Although the park facilities are a bit neglected, the experience, especially for children, is fantastic. Admission prices for foreigners are rather expensive, at 10 CUC per adult and 7 CUC per child (over 2 years old). The price for locals is just 10 pesos (MN). Definitely try your best to finagle a Cuban entrance ticket.

The Local Zoos

Of all the mainstream, family-oriented entertainment options in the city, visiting the zoo is probably the most popular for Havana locals. So popular, in fact, that there are actually two zoos in Havana. The *Jardin Zoologico de la Habana* is located in the Nuevo Vedado district, at the corner of Ave. 26 and Ave. Zoologico. While some areas of this zoo look aged, overall this facility is surprisingly modern and well maintained. There is a wide selection of exotic animals, such as zebras, lions, crocodiles, and monkeys. Most of the animals are housed in large cages or pens. The admission price is only 2 pesos (MN) for locals and 2 CUC for foreigners.

For a more natural wildlife experience, there is the *Parque Zoológico Nacional*, located in the southern suburb of Boyeros (near the Jose Marti Airport). In this sprawling park you will find hundreds of different animals, and most of them will be roaming free. The nature reserve is huge, covering over 500 hectares, but there is a free trolley bus that operates all day, offering a tour of the grounds. The price of admission is only 3 CUC and the address is Carretera de Capdevila, km 31/2, Boyeros. Hours of operation are 9am-3:30pm Wed-Sun

Explore Havana in a Guided Taxi Tour of the City

One of the easiest ways to get an overview of the different neighborhoods in Havana and to see daily life outside of the major tourist areas is to take a guided taxi tour of the city. You get to explore areas of the city and the Havana suburbs which are rarely seen by tourists. If you are staying in a hotel, you can usually book a taxi tour at the front desk. These tours will usually cost about 70 to 80 CUC per carload.

A cheaper alternative is to book a Havana taxi tour on the website www.BestCubaGuide.com/Tour. For 50 CUC per carload, you get a 2 hour tour of Havana and the suburbs, with an English speaking guide, in a modern, air conditioned vehicle. You will see many of the locations mentioned in this guidebook, and there is ample time to stop for photos, sightseeing and tasting local foods at popular markets. Refer to the website for a full tour itinerary and to make your reservation.

Night Clubs

No Havana guide would be complete without mentioning the discos and dance clubs in the city. At most of these locations you will be able to drink and practice your dance moves with locals and foreigners alike, without having to spend a lot of money. But it's very important to note that the atmosphere in some of the clubs is not for everybody. At some locations, particularly the ones most popular with foreigners, there is a high concentration of *jineteras* and *jineteros*. It's a part of life in the city that most people have come to accept. Furthermore, it's important to understand that your experiences at these locations will be highly dependant on how careful and responsible you are. Although Havana is a safe city, you will be an easy target for scam artists if you are drunk and/or flamboyantly foreign. Always exercise moderation and never run bar tabs. Most discos and bars open at about 10pm and close at around 3 or 4am.

The following is a list of the best known clubs and a synopsis of what to expect at each.

Fabrica de Arte Cubano FAC (Calle 26 at the corner of 11th, Vedado, Havana)

Opened in early 2014, this art gallery / music venue / bar / night club became an overnight sensation. It was founded by a group of local artists who wanted to create a space where regular people could be drawn into the art scene and experience Cuban culture from a new perspective. By mixing art, live music, cheap drinks and high quality

195

food, all under the roof of a remodeled former olive oil factory, the Cuban Art Factory was born. The crowd is mostly locals. The vibe is young and trendy. The dress code is casual chic (No baggy pants or running shoes). The entrance fee is 2 CUC. Drink prices, including cocktails are about 2 CUC each. The venue is open from Thursday to Sunday, 8pm until 3am. If you want to skip the long lineups, it is best to arrive early.

Casa de la Musica Habana (Ave. de Italia, near the corner of Neptuno - Central Havana)

This is a salsa dance club with a stage for shows and special performances. On most nights, especially Thursdays and Fridays, the majority of patrons are local Cubans looking to dance and meet people. If your goal is just to dance and have fun, this is the time to visit. On Wednesday nights, after 11pm, this location deviates from its usual theme and caters to the tourist crowd. Modern American pop music is played and the clientele is composed mainly of foreigners and *jineteras*. If your goal is to dance salsa in a relaxed, welcoming atmosphere, don't go on Wednesday nights. Entrance cost varies by night, but is usually about 2 to 5 CUC. Locals pay 50 pesos (MN). On most evenings, there is a matinee dance show which runs from 5pm to 9pm. This is particularly popular with locals.

Casa de la Musica Miramar (Ave. 20 at the corner of 35, Miramar)

This club is very similar to the Havana location with the exception that it is slightly more modern and upscale. While still popular with locals, its proximity to many embassies and hotels makes it a popular destination for foreigners. Naturally, this will attract jineteras. Despite that, if you go on a weeknight, the crowd will be decidedly more Cuban with a lot more dancing. Entrance is usually about 5 CUC, but is cheaper for the Matinee shows which take place from 5pm to 9pm.

Salon Rojo (21, between N and O, Vedado)

This disco caters mostly to the foreign crowd. The busiest nights are Thursdays and Fridays. Music is mostly American pop and there is very little dancing. Entrance is usually 10 CUC for foreigners, but if you arrive past midnight on a slow night, you can usually just walk inside without paying anything.

El Turquino (Corner of 23 and L, on the 25th floor of the Habana Libre Hotel)

This disco has wrap-around windows offering a gorgeous panoramic view of Havana. On certain occasions the roof is also uncovered to offer a view of the night sky. Live salsa music is played on most Monday, Tuesday, Thursday and Saturday nights. Given that the entrance cost is a bit higher than average, ranging from 10 to 20 CUC depending on the night and the musical performance, it tends to draw more foreigners than locals.

Club Rio (*El Johnny*) (Corner Calle A and 3ra, Miramar)

This venue tends to play international and modern Cuban dance music. The clientele is mostly young, college-age locals, with more foreigners showing up on Saturday nights. Entrance costs 5 CUC for foreigners and 50 pesos (MN) for locals.

La Cecilia (5ta Avenida y 110, Miramar)

This is currently the most popular disco in Havana. It is also one of the city's largest outdoor music venues where some of the most popular bands in Cuba regularly perform. For large events, the club will attract thousands of locals. Even if a popular band is not playing, this is the premier nighttime spot for dancing and having fun. On these *slow* nights, you can expect many more foreigners. Entrance usually costs 5 to 10 CUC. It's open Friday thru Sunday, 10pm to 3am. Since this is an outdoor venue, it is closed on rainy nights.

Diablo Tun Tun (Calle 20, corner 35, Miramar)

This is a very popular club for local Cubans, especially on Thursday, when matinee shows run from 5pm to 9pm (entrance price is 2 to 5 CUC). On other evenings, particularly for the nighttime shows starting at 11pm (entrance price 5 to 10 CUC), more foreigners tend to appear. Nevertheless, it is still one of the best and least touristy clubs in the city, playing all genres of music and frequented by some of the most popular musicians in Cuba.

Important Things to Know In Havana

How to Use a Phone in Havana

Making Local Calls

The cheapest way to make local calls is to simply use a local land-line phone. Most casas particulares have land-line phones which the guests can use free of charge. Phones located in hotel rooms can sometimes be used for local calls, but often this service is disabled. Usually the receptionist at the front desk will permit you to make local calls for free from the phones in the lobby.

You can also purchase a cheap *Tarjeta Propia* calling card. This card will allow you to use any public phone to make local calls. It is one of the most popular forms of communication on the island since public phones are often only set up to use phone cards, rather than coins. You can visit any ETECSA sales outlet to buy a *Propia* card for only 5 to 10 pesos (MN). It will entitle you to hundreds of minutes of use.

Dialing Instructions for land-line and public phones

In order to use the *Propia* card at a public phone, simply dial *166* to enter the directory, then dial the card number followed by the pin code.

- If you are calling a local land-line number then you must dial *07*, followed by the seven digit local number.

- If you are calling a cell phone number then you must dial *05*, followed by the seven digit cell phone number.

Dialing instructions using a Cuban based cell phone:

- If you are calling a local land-line number then you can simply dial the seven digit local number, without any prefixes.
- If you are calling a cell phone number then you must dial 5 first, followed by the seven digit cell phone number.

Making International Calls

In most cases, in order to reach a foreign number when dialing from Cuba you will have to dial the international call prefix number before the phone number. In Cuba, this number is 119. Although this method of calling is not exactly intuitive, it is rather easy, once you get the hang of it. Dialing 119 before the call signals that the call is international. You then dial your country code followed by the area code and phone number that you desire.

I have included a short list of examples of the most common destinations and the procedure for dialing their numbers.

Calling from Cuba to Canada or the United States: dial *119* then *1* then the area code followed by the phone number.

Calling from Cuba to Mexico: dial *119*, then *52*, then the area code followed by the phone number.

Calling from Cuba to Europe: Dial *119*, then the country code, then the area code followed by the phone number.

Preparing For the Weekends

Most of the tips in this section could be applicable when visiting any country in the world, but this reminder will be especially important and useful in saving you time and hassle while in Havana.

I always suggest that you complete all errands during the week, preferably before Thursday, as, during the weekend, stores, markets, banks and CADECAs will be packed with people. Furthermore, the staff at these establishments is usually reduced on the weekends, and operating hours are shortened. If you only have a few days to enjoy the city, you will certainly not want to spend 2 hours on a Saturday morning waiting in line to exchange money.

Remember the following tips:

- Try to avoid exchanging money on the weekends, as the lineups will be huge.

- Markets will be overcrowded and the supply of some food items will dwindle by noon. Shop at these places during the week or at least very early in the morning.

- If you do not already have a casa particular booked, do that before the weekend. In Havana, the most popular day for foreigners to arrive is Saturday, and the best casas will get booked quickly.

- If you need to top up your calling card or put credit on your Cuban cell phone, do it during the week, to avoid huge weekend lines.

- The internet will be slow and lineups to use the computer terminals will be longer on the weekends.

- For some very popular restaurants (mostly tourist ones) you may need to make a reservation, or be prepared to wait in a long line if dining late on Friday or Saturday nights.

- With the influx of weekend shoppers, even state stores and supermarkets sometimes run out of basic goods. Toilet paper is one item that can be very hard to find on weekends. Be sure you have what you need to get through the weekend before the weekend starts.

Hospital Locations

Local Clinics and Home Offices

Wherever you are in Cuba, a doctor will never be far away. In a large city, like Havana, you can find a neighborhood clinic or home-based family doctor's office every few city blocks. Most home offices are indicated with small signs near the front door of the house. These locations are best for treating minor ailments such as coughs, fevers, cuts and scrapes. If you cannot find a local clinic (*Policlínico*) in your area, just ask any local where the nearest family doctor lives (*casa del medico*). At locations like these, foreigners can expect to get fast service and only pay a few CUC.

Cuban Hospitals

In Havana, the largest concentration of hospitals are located in the Vedado neighborhood, close to the University of Havana. The main medical hub is situated on Calle 29, between E and G. The street is lined with large, specialized hospitals catering to all age groups and ailments. The following is a list of several hospitals in that area, which will also take foreign patients, usually at a nominal cost.

Fructuoso Rodriguez Hospital (Corner 29 and G - Entrance on F)

This is a large orthopedic hospital, treating all age groups. Many doctors in this facility have special training to treat infants and young children. The hospital looks dated, but most of the facilities are modern.

Vedado Children's Clinic (27 at the corner of F)

A large, modern facility. It is often crowded with local Cubans and it can be difficult to get rapid service.

Calixto Garcia Hospital (27 de Noviembre, near the corner of J)

This is the largest general hospital in Havana, with a campus occupying the equivalent area of 5 city blocks. The facilities and most of the quarters are modern. The service is generally highly rated.

Hospital for Foreigners

Clínica Central Cira García (Calle 20 at the corner of Ave. 41, Playa)

This hospital is located in the Playa neighborhood of Havana, close to many large hotels and foreign embassies. The service is almost exclusively catered towards foreigners. The facility is very modern and rarely crowded. The prices for medical procedures are high, as compared to other hospitals in the city, but if you have comprehensive medical insurance, then this is definitely the place to come for the best service and treatment.

Trinidad Bonus Section

Trinidad is a small town, located on the south coast of Cuba, near the midpoint of the island. It is one of the oldest towns in Cuba, with a history dating back more than 500 years. The town is very well preserved, with mostly original architecture, tight, winding streets, paved with cobblestones, and a picturesque surrounding of hills, valleys, farms and even a nearby beach. It is one of the most popular excursion destinations for tourists visiting Havana.

State organized bus tours, usually lasting a day or two are offered by many Cuban tour operators and can be purchased in most hotel lobbies. Official excursion prices range from about 200 CUC to over 400 CUC per person, depending on the duration and itinerary of the trip. With a little bit of planning, you can organize your own Trinidad excursion for considerably less. If you are eager to view a charming, old world town that has been listed as a UNESCO World Heritage site since 1988, then Trinidad is the place to go.

Getting From Havana to Trinidad

<u>Taking the Bus</u>

Despite being 365 kilometers (225 miles) away from Havana, it is relatively easy to get to Trinidad, even for a novice traveler. You can easily take the Viazul bus service, which operates daily routes from Havana to Trinidad. If you book ahead of time, you will have no problem getting a seat. The Viazul bus terminal in Havana is located at the corner of Avenida 26 and Avenida Zoologico, in the Nuevo Vedado neighborhood. You can book your tickets directly at the terminal, and it is advised to book at least a few days before traveling. An even better option is to book and pay for your tickets online, at www.Viazul.com. On the day of travel, you simply arrive at the bus terminal 30 minutes before your departure time to check your bags (if you are traveling with luggage) and you will soon be seated in a modern, air conditioned bus, making your way towards your destination. The bus ride costs 25 CUC per person and the trip takes about 6 hours. The bus makes stops at most major towns along the way to drop off and take on new passengers. This is the main reason for the extended trip duration. Once in Trinidad, the bus terminal is just beside the town center, within easy walking distance to most popular locations.

Hire a Taxi

Hiring a taxi to get you from Havana to Trinidad is more expensive than taking the bus, but the advantage is that you can set your own departure schedule and your travel time is reduced significantly, with most taxis making the direct trip in 4 hours or less. Your taxi options are varied and depend on what kind of trip you want to experience and how many other passengers you are traveling with. Taxis always charge by the carload, so it is more affordable to share the ride with other tourists and split the fare accordingly.

A yellow, air conditioned, modern taxi car will usually make the trip from Havana to Trinidad for about 160 CUC. This is the most convenient option for most people. Shared between 4 passengers, this would only be marginally more expensive than the Viazul. There are also old American car taxis which do the trip for roughly the same price. The disadvantage with these vehicles is that they are not air conditioned, and the windows are usually rolled all the way down for the duration of the trip, for ventilation. For a long distance trip like this, it can become unpleasant. Furthermore, as these vehicles are old, there is an increased risk of breakdown on the highway. If you are traveling as a larger group, you can also consider hiring a minibus to take your group to Trinidad. An air conditioned minibus can usually seat 10 to 14 passengers and the trip price ranges from 220 CUC to 300 CUC total.

<u>Finding A Taxi</u>

It is likely that any taxi you see in Havana would be willing to quote you a price to drive to Trinidad. If you are looking for a better deal, a good place to search is near the Viazul terminal in Havana (corner of Avenida 26 and Avenida Zoologico, in the Nuevo Vedado neighborhood). There are usually dozens of taxis waiting outside the bus station anxious for long distance fares. If you are traveling alone, these drivers will even help to find other tourists to share the ride and the cost.

If you are planning your trip to Trinidad ahead of time, you can book your taxi online, at <u>www.BestCubaGuide.com/Taxis</u>. The website offers some of the lowest prices available with many different vehicle and trip options. A modern, air conditioned taxi, from Havana to Trinidad, with up to 4 passengers, is only 160 CUC, with door to door pickup and drop-off. In low season the price is even lower.

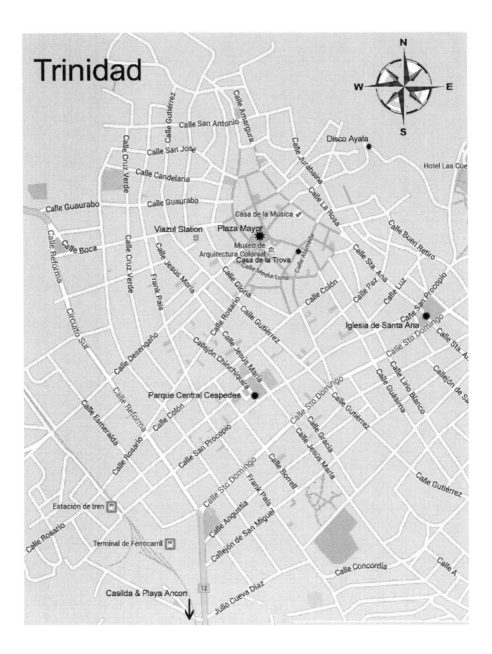

Trinidad

Calle Gutiérrez
Calle San Antonio
Calle Amargura
Calle San José
Calle Cruz Verde
Calle Candelaria
Calle Aurabaina
Disco Ayala
Hotel Las Cue
Calle Guaurabo
Calle Guaurabo
Calle La Rosa
Casa de la Música
Viazul Station
Plaza Mayor
Calle Buen Retiro
Calle Reforma
Calle Boca
Calle Cruz Verde
Museo de
Arquitectura Colonial
Casa de la Trova
Calle Meola Luna
Calle Sta. Ana
Calle Paz
Calle Luz
Calle Jesús María
Frank País
Calle Alameda
Calle Colón
Calle San Procopio
Calle Gloria
Calle Rosario
Calle Gutiérrez
Iglesia de Santa Ana
Calle Sto Domingo
Calle Sta. A
Circuito Sur
Calle Desengaño
Callejón Chinchiquirá
Calle Jesús María
Calle Reforma
Calle Lino Blanco
Callejón de S
Parque Central Cespedes
Calle Guásima
Calle Esmeralda
Calle Reforma
Calle Colón
Calle Sto Domingo
Calle Gutiérrez
Calle Rosario
Calle San Procopio
Calle Gracia
Calle Jesús María
Calle Gutiérrez
Estación de tren
Calle Sto Domingo
Frank País
Calle Borrell
Calle Rosario
Terminal de Ferrocarril
Calle Angustia
Callejón de San Miguel
Calle Concordia
Calle A
Casilda & Playa Ancon
12
Julio Cueva Díaz

Exploring the Town of Trinidad

<u>Old Town</u>

The Trinidad town center is commonly referred to as the Old Town. It is very easy to identify and most foreigners who visit Trinidad spend most of their time in this area. The streets are paved in uneven cobblestones. The houses and buildings are almost all hundreds of years old. This was the the first part of the town which was constructed when the area was originally settled, over 500 years ago. It has been well preserved and over the years many of the buildings have been carefully restored. There are strict preservation laws enacted by the Cuban government to ensure that any renovations to the buildings within this area maintain the architectural integrity of the original structures. Effectively, the Old Town is a giant museum, and this is what makes it such a strong tourist draw. The Old Town is also gated off to vehicle traffic. Only walking and biking is permitted.

The streets in the Old Town are tight and winding, to a foreigner it can seem chaotic. Despite the small overall area of this neighborhood (less than 500 meters in diameter) it is very easy to become disoriented and lost. This plan was by design, in order to confuse and impede pirates, which regularly invaded the town throughout the 17th century.

The Old Town is built on a gently sloping hill. At the center of town, located near the top of the hill, is the Plaza Mayor, the central town square. The plaza is surrounded by dozens of historically significant buildings, most of which have been converted to museums. If you enjoy history, you will find this an ideal location to explore. In front of the plaza is the imposing Church of the Holy Trinity (Iglesia Parroquial de la Santísima Trinidad). To the right of the church (one block north of the plaza) is the Church and Convent of Saint Francis (Iglesia y Convento de San Francisco). This church, with its tall, brightly painted bell tower is one of Trinidad's most recognizable landmarks, prominently featured on advertisements and postcards, as well as on Cuba's 25 cent CUC coin. Also in the area you will see several outdoor street fairs where local sellers have set up stalls selling crafts, linens, souvenirs and clothes.

Eastern Trinidad

Walking south-east, out of the gated Old Town, you will soon be entering a decidedly poorer area. Although the streets are still paved with cobblestones, you will notice cars driving over them and a lot fewer tourists. Most of the houses in this area maintain the same architecture as those in the Old Town, but lack restoration.

This neighborhood of eastern Trinidad is a great area to explore if you want to get away from the tourist crowds and see how the locals live. The most prominent attraction in the area is the Iglesia de Santa Ana, facing a large square (Plaza Santa Ana). The church is in ruins, but there is a small museum and restaurant/bar nearby. The square has historical significance, as the former location of a large Spanish prison.

The streets in eastern Trinidad all gently slope away from the Old Town and towards the ocean, which, on a clear day, can be seen in the distance. The small port town of Casilda, located about 4 kilometers south of Trinidad, connected by a small highway, can also be seen.

New Town

If you are entering Trinidad by taxi or bus, then the first neighborhood that you will likely pass through is the New Town. As the name suggests, this area is composed of mostly newer buildings, which are not as architecturally ornate as anything in the rest of the city. If you do not have a fixed destination in mind when arriving in Trinidad, it is common for taxi drivers to drop you off at the Parque Central Cespedes. This is a small plaza, located in front of the Iberostar Grand Hotel Trinidad, (one of the most prominent hotels in the city). This area is generally considered as the border between the New Town and the beginning of the Old Town.

While there is not much of historic importance located in the newer part of town, it can be a good place to explore and people watch, as this is where the vast majority of locals live and spend their days. Street food vendors and small paladares also line the main streets in this area and prices for food and drinks are a fraction of what you will pay in the Old Town. If only for that, it is well worth spending some time in this neighborhood.

Note: Trinidad's street hustlers (jineteros) are notorious for their brazenness, persistence and organization. The situation is far worse here than anywhere else in Cuba, including Havana. It is highly advisable to be suspicious of anybody you meet on the street offering you assistance or advice relating to bars, restaurants, entertainment options or casas particulares. They almost certainly have an angle where they will be able to scam a bit of money out of you by the end of the day. Although these scams are generally harmless and petty, they can be tedious, time consuming and off-putting. One of the most common scams occurs when tourists have just arrived in the town and are searching for their pre-booked accommodations. Hustlers wait at the Viazul terminal and greet unsuspecting tourists, as they exit the bus. They explain, usually in well spoken English, that they were sent by the casa owner to escort the tourist directly to their casa. Inevitably, if you follow one of these hustlers, you will arrive at an entirely different casa than that which you booked, and the hustler will always make a healthy commission from your misfortune. The hustlers are so well versed in their trade that they sometimes even scam Cuban taxi drivers who might get lost in Trinidad's winding streets, convincing the drivers to drop off tourists at the wrong casas. Always confirm that the casa you are staying in, is in fact the actual casa that you made reservations for. And, if you meet somebody at the bus station who claims to be sent from your casa landlord, never tell them your name and casa details first. If they were genuinely sent from the landlord to escort you to the casa, make them confirm your details first.

Casas Particulares in Trinidad

As Trinidad is a very popular tourist destination, and has been for many years, there is an abundance of good casas particulares throughout the town. In the historic center of Trinidad many of the rental units are located inside historic mansions. These mansions retain most of their old world architectural details, including stone columns, vaulted ceilings, wooden beams and moldings, and expansive inner courtyards allowing natural light and fresh cross breezes to flow. In these mansions, while you have a private room with its own locking door, you will often share the common areas of the house with the landlords and other guests.

Outside of the town center, the rental properties tend to be newer. These casas are often independent rooms or apartments, where you receive the key to the front door and can come and go in complete privacy.

Regardless of the age of the casa particular, they almost always have air conditioned bedrooms with modern, en-suite bathrooms. Furthermore, most casas have rooftop terraces which offer picturesque views of the city and surrounding mountains.

There are enough casas in Trinidad that a reservation is usually not necessary. You can simply arrive in the town, walk around for a few minutes and locate a suitable place to stay. The rental properties are all clearly marked with signs above their doors. Even if one landlord does not have vacancy, they will quickly call up friends and find a nearby place for you to stay.

If you want to book accommodations ahead of time, you can search online. There is also a good selection of rental properties on the website www.BestCubaGuide.com

Note: You might arrive in Trinidad and wonder why there are so many elegant mansions in such a small town, located rather far from

Havana. While the abundance of tourism is currently driving the Trinidad economy, there are also some very important historical factors for the high relative wealth in the region. As one of the earliest settlements in Cuba, and surrounded by fertile farmland, Trinidad was the nexus for the island's early sugar industry. Years later, pottery and clay tile manufacturing boosted economic activity. And in present day, tobacco processing is a major industry throughout the area.

Getting Around

Trinidad is a rather small town, less than 2.5 kms (1.5 miles) wide. The easiest way to get around the main areas is on foot. Within the historic center, no cars are permitted, so walking is the norm. Bikes are also used, but given that the streets are paved in rounded cobblestones, biking can be challenging (most casas particulares can arrange bike rentals at a cost of about 3 to 5 CUC per day). Even walking on the cobblestones can get tiring, and as such, many streets have a narrow cement sidewalk along the side, which, despite being crowded, is often the best option.

In the newer parts of town, the streets are asphalt and accommodate bikes and cars. Bicycle taxis are abundant and can take you from one end of town to the other for about 3 CUC.

If you have a bike, you can easily use it to get to visit some of the interesting locations outside of the main town (these are listed on the following pages). Yellow taxis are also plentiful and are the quickest way to visit places on the outskirts of town. There are also some communal taxis which operate routes to the local attractions. While these are cheaper than yellow taxis, they can be difficult to locate. Lastly, there are tour buses which have regular routes from Trinidad to the surroundings. Mostly these are reserved for foreigners who have booked excursion packages. Sometimes there are extra seats available at affordable fares. You can visit one of the many tourist information offices located throughout Trinidad or ask your casa landlord for help in making the reservations.

There is also a restored steam train which operates in the area. This will be discussed in the following section.

Interesting Places to Visit and Things to do in the Surround Areas

Casilda - This is a small port town located about 5 minutes driving distance south of Trinidad. You can easily get there by taxi, bike or walking. The town overlooks the Bay of Casilda, which is a popular area for snorkeling and a good place to find an outfitter, if you want to go sport fishing. The town itself is modest, although there are a few rental properties and a couple of restaurants. Casilda is a good place to stay if you want to experience Trinidad from a less touristy perspective, while also being closer to the ocean.

Playa Ancon - On the other side of the Bay of Casilda is the lovely Playa Ancon beach. The beach is located on a long archipelago that shields the bay. The road leading to the beach, from Casilda, sweeps around the bay. All told, Playa Ancon is about 10 minutes driving distance from Trinidad. You would be able to bike there in about 30 minutes. The beach is sandy, wide, and about 8 kms (5 miles) long. There are three large resort hotels along the beach, located at about the midpoint of the archipelago. But on either side of those hotels, there are vast expanses of relatively secluded beach, offering tranquility and seclusion. It is very easy to find a hidden, private area on Playa Ancon, and you could easily spend a day in the sun, sand and surf without seeing another person.

Valle de los Ingenios - East of Trinidad you will find the sprawling Valle de los Ingenios (Valley of the Sugar Mills). Originally, this area was the epicenter of Cuba's sugar-trade economy. Currently, the lush valley is spotted with the ruins of dozens of sugar mills, abandoned sugar warehouses and historic colonial manors and slave dwellings. The best way to see the valley is with a horseback riding tour which your casa landlord will be able to organize. Prices are approximately 20 CUC for 5 to 6 hour tour, covering most important sightseeing locations.

El Mirador Restaurant - About 5 kms (3 miles) east of Trinidad, along the Circuito Sur highway, is the El Mirador restaurant / bar. The establishment is perched on a hill and offers 360 degree views of the Valle de los Ingenios (Valley of the Sugar Mills). Drinks are cheap and food is moderately prices, but it is completely free to simply walk up the long flight of stairs to the restaurant and enjoy the views of the valley from the open terrace. It will definitely give you some perspective on the grandiosity of the area and the importance that sugar production once had for Cuba's economy.

Antique Train - A fun way to experience the valley is to take a ride on the antique steam train. The train departs from Trinidad and slowly makes its way through the valley, going through several tunnels and over a few iron bridges, eventually stopping at the famous Manaca Iznaga estate and the hacienda Guachinango, which will be discussed in the next section. Although a ride on this antique engine is enjoyable, the train is highly unreliable. The train has scheduled departures every day, leaving Trinidad at 9:30am and returning at 2pm. This changes often, due to breakdowns and weather events. Round trip tickets costs 10 CUC and can be purchased directly at the train station in Trinidad, located at the intersection of Calle Antonio Guiteras and General Lino Perez, in the western end of the town.

Manaca Iznaga Estate - Continuing east, along the Ciruito Sur highway a further 10 kms from the El Mirador lookout, you will find the Manaca Iznaga estate. The 18th century plantation was owned by Pedro Iznaga, one of the richest men in Cuba who made his fortune mostly in slave trafficking. The estate is well preserved and one of the most popular sightseeing destinations in the area. The main draw is the Iznaga Tower, which is 45 meters tall. It was used to oversee the slaves in the plantation and as a symbol of the Iznaga family's power and wealth. Originally the tower had a large bell at the top. This bell is now on display at the base of the tower. The cost to walk up to the top of the tower is 1 CUC. The colonial Iznaga estate house faces the tower and has been converted into a restaurant. Also on the estate grounds are some slave dwellings in original condition. Most

215

of the small houses beside the estate were former slave dwellings which have since been renovated and are currently occupied by town locals. The antique steam train has a stop just beside the estate.

Hacienda Guachinango - This is a well preserved plantation ranch-house which currently operates as a restaurant. It is located in the valley, about 2 kms away from the Manaca Iznaga estate. It is surrounded by lush farmland and there is a small river (Río Ay) that winds through the surrounding fields. The antique steam train stops directly in front of the house every morning. You can easily walk to the Manaca Iznaga estate, along the train track, in about 30 minutes.

Topes de Collantes - About 5 kms northwest of Trinidad, connected by the Circuito Sur highway, is the massive Topes de Collantes natural reserve park which encompasses the Escambray Mountain range. Within the park, the main attractions are caves, waterfalls, clear blue lakes and rivers and there is ample opportunity for hiking and to see indigenous plants and wildlife. Given the unpredictable weather in the mountains and the steep sloping roads, special vehicles are required to drive to the highest attractions in the park. Certain taxi drivers will offer to make the trip for an additional fee, but breakdowns are common. It is best to visit with an organized excursion. Accommodations within the reserve are also available, at a reasonable cost.

Trinidad Nightlife

Casa de la Musica - An outdoor music and dance venue, located on a steep, sloping street, just off the Plaza Mayor in the Old Town. Drinks are cheap and the music plays day and night. There are tables and chairs scattered around, and many people simply sit on the steps leading up the hill. The atmosphere is very relaxed and offers a good chance to meet up with locals and practice your dance steps. There is no entrance fee. Just walk around and enjoy yourself.

Casa de la Trova - Located one block east of the Plaza Mayor, this indoor music and dance hall hosts nightly shows with popular Cuban musical groups. There is a large outdoor terrace, usually filled with locals and tourists. The entrance fee is 1 CUC for foreigners.

Disco Ayala - Located about 6 blocks northeast of the Plaza Mayor, on a small hill, beside the Hotel Las Cuevas, just on the outskirts of town. Disco Ayala is a large nightclub built inside a natural cave. Enjoy salsa and reggaeton as you dance the night away in this cavernous setting. The entrance fee is 3 CUC and includes 1 drink.

Top Ten Cuba Tip List!

1) Always negotiate prices. As a foreigner in a relatively poor city, most of the local merchants will see you as a cash machine. If you are taking a taxi, buying a bike, browsing souvenirs or renting a casa particular; whenever you request a price for a product or service, vendors will immediately throw out a high number. Do not feel shy about making a low counter offer. You can sometimes save 50% or more. Most importantly, don't worry about walking away from a vendor if the asking price for something is too high. This tactic will almost certainly sway the seller to become more reasonable, as most vendors hate losing sales.

2) In conjunction with tip #1: If you act like a tourist, you will be treated like a tourist. If you walk down a busy tourist street wearing a novelty panama hat and Che Guevara t-shirt, speaking English loudly and carrying a large SLR camera, every *jinetero* in Havana will approach you to strike-up a conversation. It's not necessarily a bad thing, but you will be hounded by money-seekers constantly. Regardless of your color, nationality or language, you are far more likely to blend in as a local if you simply dress modestly, similarly to how you would dress on a daily basis in your home country.

3) Be safe. The best way to do this is to exercise caution and common sense. A general rule is that if you would not do something in your own country, then you should not risk doing it in Cuba either. For foreigners, the risk of running into trouble increases dramatically when heavy drinking is involved. Moderation and good judgment will help you avoid most hassles and ensure a problem free trip.

4) Use Moneda Nacional. Most Cubans receive their salary in Moneda Nacional and this is the most common currency used. There is no reason that you cannot use it as well. For some goods and services you will have no choice but to use CUC. This is especially the case in a large city like Havana. But this should be the exception

and not the rule. If you make an effort to only buy things which are priced in MN you will save a lot of money. Furthermore, you will immerse yourself in the Cuban lifestyle, since you will be visiting the same stores and shops as locals.

5) Treat yourself to a good, sit down meal every day. While you can survive well in Havana by simply eating street food, it is a good idea to have something slightly more fulfilling at least once per day. A full meal at a restaurant only costs about 4 CUC, and the generous serving of healthy food will give you the energy that you need to explore every inch of Havana. Despite being delicious, most street food in Cuba is simply filled with empty carbohydrates and provides little nutrition.

6) Appreciate the culture. Cuba is really different from a lot of other places in the world. You will especially notice this if you are from a modern, western country. In Cuba, people have different attitudes towards money, family, community and entertainment. Observing the locals and making a few friends will really help you to understand the Cuban way of life.

7) Keep an open mind and let go of any pre-conceived notions about Cuba or Havana. Contrary to some claims, everything is not all about politics. The average Cuban is well-informed of the broad themes affecting their country and the world. At the same time, they are probably far less concerned with these matters than you would think. While the most vocal members of society will immediately share their opinions, that does not mean that they speak for everybody. If you talk to a variety of regular people, you are sure to gain a clearer perspective.

8) Explore everything. Most guidebooks provide lists of hundreds of different tourist attractions to visit. While these places can help you learn history and facts, they give you almost no insight into daily life. The best way to discover Cuba is to leave your map at home and simply get lost as you wander around. Cuban culture is very open, and you are almost guaranteed to meet people and see fascinating

things as you walk around. In Havana, this is especially true. If a door is unlocked, you should consider that an invitation to enter.

9) Don't get bogged down by small problems. In Cuba, inconveniences are normal. Buses will break down, reservations will be changed, lines will be long. The sun will burn you. The weather will make you sweat and the mosquitoes will make you itch. In Havana particularly, you might even get scammed out of a few dollars, despite your best efforts to avoid it. Don't take these problems personally; they happen to foreigners and locals alike. Don't allow them to sour your trip, or your image of the country.

10) Enjoy the cheap entertainment. There are a lots of fun things to do in Havana, and most of them are either completely free, or cost just a nominal price. If the average local, earning just $30 per month, can find ways to have fun, then you can surely keep yourself entertained on a tight budget. Don't always expect to go someplace specific and engage in a particular activity for amusement. In Cuba, the greatest pleasures come from relaxing and interacting with interesting people. Consider this an opportunity to slow down your life and enjoy the moment, rather than simply jumping from one plan to another.

The Real Havana: Cheap Casa Particular Guide

The following is a list of some of the best and cheapest casas particulares in Havana. They are all located within the Vedado neighborhood, as this is, in my opinion, the best neighborhood to stay in. All prices are in CUC per night. There are no supplementary costs for having extra guests stay in the room. As mentioned before, all rental properties in Cuba undergo strict government inspections and meet high quality standards. I have personally stayed at all the properties in this list and I can confirm that they are all fantastic locations, certain to further your experience in Havana by allowing you to live like a local and save money.

The rental properties in the following section are part of the Real Havana network. Special, low rates have been negotiated with the landlords. There are no middleman commissions to pay at these casas. This will potentially save you hundreds of dollars in brokerage fees.

More casa listings, as well as photos for all the casas listed in this guide, can be found on the websites www.BestCubaGuide.com .

You can use this website to reserve the casas particulares directly, online, at no additional cost.

If you are contacting the casas particulares by phone, be sure to mention that you saw their listing in the Real Havana guide, in order to get the special low pricing.

Private Rooms

The following accommodations are for private rooms within a shared, enclosed house. The guests have the use of some common areas, such as the living room, balcony/terrace and kitchen facilities, and have exclusive private use of their own room, which has a lock on the door. In many cases, the guest will also be given a key to the main entrance of the house so he or she can enter and exit at will, without having to disturb the house owner. Some houses rent a single room, while others rent two or more. These can be rented out all together, for people traveling in groups, or separately, for single travelers and couples. All rooms, by Cuban law, must have a window and air conditioner or fan. Most rooms also have a private fridge, an en-suite bathroom and offer either a private or shared telephone line. In all cases, Cuban guests are permitted to enter, free of charge. Sometimes they are asked to sign a guestbook to ensure the safety of both the landlord and the tenant. Specific details for each casa are provided below.

1) <u>Casa Tomasa:</u> Calle C #558 Altos, entre 23 y 25. Tel (537) 833 1266
Two rooms for rent, each with a fridge and air conditioner. Very modern and spacious rooms (200 sq.ft) located inside a restored mansion, offering a host of modern amenities. The house has a huge, sun-filled terrace in front, located just in front of a large park and only 50 feet away from La Rampa. Landlord asks 35 CUC per night, per room.

2) <u>Casa Villa Margarita:</u> Calle 27 # 510, e/ E y F. Tel (537) 831 1744, Cell (53)5 826 3891
The casa particular offers 2 large bedrooms, each with their own living rooms and modern, en-suite bathroom. It is the perfect place for a couple to enjoy a nice relaxing time in Havana. Each room has air conditioning as well. Guests receive the keys and can come and go as they want. At the back of the house there is a massive covered terrace space with chairs, tables and hammocks for relaxing. There is

also parking for vehicles if needed. Landlord asks 30 to 35 CUC per night, per room.

3) Casa Carlos and Julio: Calle E #609 Altos, entre 25 y 27. Tel (537) 832 7203
Three large rooms available. In addition to their private quarters, guests have access to a front room, filled with plants and artwork, and a well-equipped kitchen. This apartment is located on the second floor of a mansion and the owners live on the third floor. The owners are always available to offer advice or tips on exploring the city, but mostly you will have complete privacy. All rooms have en-suite bathrooms which are huge and modern. Plants fill the apartment and give a natural warmth and charm. Landlord asks 35 CUC per night, per room.

4) Casa Leo and Ivelis: Calle 23 #608 bajos, entre E y F. Tel (537)832 0071, Cell 53(5)332 5639 or 53(5)332 5237
This casa offers two large, first floor rooms within a huge, modernly decorated mansion. Guests also have access to a private living area measuring over 300 sq.ft and a shared entertainment room with a large, flat panel television and sound system. In addition, there is a terrace in the front of the mansion. The landlord, Ivelis, is an English professor in Havana who is always available to answer questions or give advice about the city. Landlord asks 30 CUC per night.

5) Casa Palacio (Ydalmis): Calle Jovellar #264, altos, entre Infanta y N. Tel (537)879 5647, Cell, (53)5 290 3318
The casa particular offers 2 large bedrooms, each with their own modern, en-suite bathroom. It is the perfect place for a couple to enjoy a nice relaxing time in Havana. Each room has modern, silent, wall mounted air conditioner. One bedroom has a queen bed. The other bedroom has a king bed. There are also 2 terraces in the front of the casas which overlook the street and offer city views. Landlord asks 30 to 35 CUC per night.

6) Casa Guido: Calle C #354, Apartment C, entre 15 y 17. Tel (537)832 5606
This casa particular offers 3 large bedrooms, each with their own en-suite bathroom and modern, silent air conditioner. There is a huge living room and dining room in the casa, as well as a terrace. Guests receive the keys and can come and go as they want. The landlord lives in an adjacent apartment and gives his guests complete privacy, but is available to answer questions or to assists in any way possible. Many meal options are also available. Landlord asks 35 to 40 CUC per night. Deals available if you rent the whole casa.

7) Casa Alexander and Margarita - Private Rooms: Calle 25 #806 entre B y C. Cell 53(5)268 5506
Be a guest in this massive colonial mansion! There are two very large (over 250 sq.ft), second floor rooms to rent, each with its own bathroom and fridge. The rooms can be rented together or separately. There is a large terrace which is reserved exclusively for guests, as well as a private living room area. Alexander lives on the far side of the mansion, and offers a lot of privacy to his guests, but is always available to answer questions or give advice. Guests receive the keys upon their arrival and can come and go as they please. Alexander also has a vehicle and can offer city tours, taxi services and economical transportation to the countryside or other Cuban provinces. Some English is spoken. Landlord asks 40 CUC per night, per room.

8) Casa Alicia: Calle F #104, entre 5 y Calzada. Tel (537)832 0671, Cell 53(5)297 4748
This casa particular offers 3 large bedrooms, each with modern en-suite bathrooms. There is also a large living room and dining area which guests can use. There is air conditioning in each room. Total capacity for the casa is 8 people. Two of the bedrooms have mezzanines for extra space. The ceilings are very high! The casa is perfect if you are traveling with children or as a group of 3 or more people. Landlord asks 35 to 40 CUC per night, per room.

9) Casa Maribel: Calle B #712 entre 29 y Zapata. Tel (537)831 3875, Cell 53(5)315 3922

Two large, first floor rooms for rent within a restored colonial mansion. Both rooms are about 150 sq.ft and are equipped with televisions, air conditioners and fridges. Guests have the use of a small outdoor terrace at the rear of the building and a large yard and terrace in the front. Maribel is a charming older woman who respects the privacy of her guests but is always available to answer questions or give advice. The rooms in this house are modern and fully equipped, and are priced very affordably, as the landlord prefers to have them rented as much as possible. Make your reservation in advance, to ensure that these rooms are available. Landlord asks only 25 CUC per night, per room.

10) Casa Gloria: Calle 23 # 551 apto 6 entre F y G, Vedado. (53) 6477677, Cell 39 338 871 1760

The casa offers 3 large rooms for rent. Each room has and en-suite bathroom and air conditioner. There are lots of windows which fill the area with natural light. Total capacity for 6 people. There is also a full kitchen and a very large living room area. The apartment offers views of the city and from the terrace on the top floor, you can relax and see the ocean. Landlord asks 35 CUC per night, per room. Prices are negotiable for stays longer than 1 week.

11) Casa Gladys: Calle D #401, esquina 17. Tel (537)836 7015

Three rooms are for rent in this massive, 2000 sq.ft, sun filled, second floor, penthouse apartment. This modernly furnished and completely renovated apartment offers a luxurious atmosphere in Vedado. The rooms can be rented separately, or the whole apartment can be rented together. Each room offers its own large and modern bathroom. A laundry machine is also available for guest use. The main living area has a gorgeous corner balcony which overlooks the intersection of Calle D and 17. Gladys is an active, middle aged woman who lives alone in the apartment and never interferes with the guests. She is almost never home, so you will basically have complete independence. Some English is spoken. Landlord asks 30 CUC per night, per room.

12) <u>Casa La Casita:</u> Calle 3ra #119, e/ D y E, Havana Vedado, Cuba (537)830 8027 Cell (+41) 319617397
The casa offers two large rooms for rent. Each room has an air conditioner and there are lots of windows which fill the area with natural light. The rooms share a common bathroom which has been recently renovated with top of the line fixtures. If you are two couples, or a couple traveling with kids, then this casa is perfect for you. Landlord asks 30 CUC per night, per room.

13) <u>Casa Particular Carlos y Martitza:</u> Calle H #513, bajo, e/ 21 y 23. (537)835 3034 Cell (535)248 9121 Cell (535)404 8383
The mansion is absolutely stunning and was completely renovated and remodeled in the last year, with top of the line furnishings. It is one of the most impressive casas in Vedado.
This casa particular offers 3 large bedrooms, each with modern en-suite bathrooms. There is also a large living room and dining area. It is the perfect place to enjoy a nice relaxing time in Havana. There is air conditioning in each room. Landlord asks 35 to 40 CUC per night, per room. Deals available for stays of 7 days or longer.

14) <u>Casa Particular Martinez:</u> Calle J #411, e/ 19 y 21, Vedado (537) 832 9008 Cell: (535) 249 3825 Cell: (535) 296 6524
This casa particular offers 2 large bedrooms, each with modern en-suite bathrooms and air conditioning. There is also a large living room and dining area. At the rear of the house there is a large outdoor space for entertaining or relaxing. There is also a long driveway that can be used to park up to 2 vehicles. Landlord asks 35 to 40 CUC per night, per room. Deals available for stays of 7 days or longer.

Independent Rooms

These casas particulares are rooms which are private and completely independent, with very limited interaction between guests and the landlord. They are not simply rooms for rent in a house - they have **their own exterior door** and guests are given the keys, so they can come and go in complete privacy. These *Independent Rooms* offer a bit more privacy than the *Private Rooms,* listed above. Cuban guests are always permitted to enter, free of charge.

1) <u>Casa Miriam:</u> Calle I #257 bajos, entre 13 y 15. Tel (537)832 7923
Two large, independent, first floor rooms for rent. Each room spans about 200 sq.ft and is modernly decorated with ample sunlight. Both rooms have a queen bed as well as a single bed. This makes it great for families traveling together, or if you plan on having guests. Each room has its own independent entrance and renters are provided all the keys, so they can enter and leave as needed, in complete privacy. The rooms can be rented together or separately. Meals are available and guests also have access to the shared kitchen area. Each room also has access to a large, private terrace and yard. A carport is also available for guest use. Landlord asks 30 CUC per room, per night.

2) <u>Casa El Bosquecito - Independent Rooms:</u> Calle C #661, entre 27 y 29 (Corner 29). Tel (537)830 4087
Two large, private, first floor rooms nestled within the grounds of a restored, colonial house. The rooms are completely independent, with their own doors to the outside. They opens onto a large terrace, surrounded by a lush garden. Both rooms have a large queen bed as well as a smaller double bed. Children are always welcome. All keys are provided so the guests can come and go as they please. The landlord, named Pello, is an older man who passes his day tending his garden and loves telling stories and sharing jokes with the guests. Landlord asks 30 CUC per night, per room.

3) <u>Casa Elvira:</u> Calle B #716, altos, entre 29 y Zapata. Tel (537)830 4682

A second floor room, located on a quiet street, only 5 minutes walking to all the action of La Rampa. The room has a queen sized bed, as well as a smaller bed for children or guests. There is also an en-suite bathroom. The landlord speaks English and a bit of French. Landlord asks 25 to 30 CUC per night.

4) <u>Casa Emma:</u> Calle K #357, entre 19 y 21. Tel (537)836 8820, Cell 53(5)322 6999

The owner rents two separate and completely private rooms, located at the back of the main house. Each room is accessible by its own private front door, opening up to a large, outside courtyard. In order to get to the courtyard and rooms, you must enter through the main house and walk through the center hallway. Although the rooms are completely private, and you are provided your own keys, you must ring the doorbell of the main house and walk through the hallway in order to get to the rooms. The owner, Emma, prefers this setup for her own safety, as she is a single woman. If you are a woman traveling alone, this casa would be ideal, because it is extremely safe while still offering complete privacy. One of the private rooms is large (about 200 sq.ft) and includes a queen bed as well as a double bed located on a mezzanine. The other room is just fractionally smaller and has no mezzanine area. Both rooms are completely modernized with new bathrooms and flat screen televisions. Landlord asks 30 CUC per night, per room.

Private Apartments

The following listings are for completely private and independent apartments which can be rented in the Vedado area. These are whole apartments, which usually have a bedroom, a private living room, dining room, kitchen, bathroom and terrace. All apartments include an air conditioner and a fridge. Most also included a kitchen and a private or shared telephone line. In all cases, Cuban guests are permitted to enter, free of charge. Details are listed in the write-ups.

1) <u>Casa Celia Bungalow:</u> Calle 15, #910, Entre 6 y 8, Vedado, Cuba. Tel. (537) 833 6832. Cell. (535) 270 5835.
This casa is located on a large, quiet property in Vedado.
The bungalow is at the back of the main house and is completely independent. Guests receive the keys and can come and go as they want. The bungalow has 1 large bedroom as well as a living room, kitchen and modern bathroom. It is the perfect place for a couple to enjoy a nice relaxing time in Havana. There is air conditioning as well. There is also a secondary, smaller, independent bungalow on the property. Landlord asks 40 CUC per night.

2) <u>Casa Vista Panorama:</u> Calle 23, No. 655, 17th floor, Apt #182, entre D y E, Vedado, Tel. (537) 830 2435 Cell. (535) 330 6898
Huge, modern apartment, located in a high rise building on La Rampa (23rd street), in Vedado. 3 large bedrooms. The apartment is located on the 17th floor and the terrace offers a panoramic view of the city of Havana and the ocean. Each bedroom has an independent, private bathroom, air conditioning, a high quality mattress. The main living area has a living room and a fully equipped, modern kitchen, with new appliances. Landlord asks 45 to 50 CUC per night.

3) <u>Casa Mary and Armando:</u> Calle J #414, Apt 28, entre 19 y 21. Tel (537)830 6374, Cell 53(5)292 4791
Very well located, second floor apartment with living room, kitchen, bar, one bedroom and en-suite bathroom. This place is modernly decorated and very private. There is also a large terrace on the first

floor. The apartment is located on the second floor of the main house and has its own independent staircase. It is rented with the keys, so you can come and go in complete privacy. Armando also has a fantastic, old American car that he uses for giving city tours. This can be arranged separately if desired. The apartment is very quiet and located just a few blocks from the Habana Libre hotel. Some English is spoken. Landlord asks 30 CUC per night.

4) Casa Gustavo: Calle 25 # 453, altos, entre J y I. Tel (537)832 1246 Cell 53(5)281 3205
A completely independent, second floor, one bedroom apartment, just steps to the University of Havana, and directly adjacent to the Biology Department. The apartment is about 400 sq.ft, offering a large living room with a kitchen, and an equally large bedroom, with en-suite bathroom. You are given the keys to the apartment and can come and go in complete privacy. It is located about 2 minutes walking distance to the Habana Libre hotel, which offers internet access and WIFI. In terms of privacy and location, this apartment has it all. Despite being close to all the action, this sunny and airy apartment is surprising quiet. There is a private phone in the apartment, as well as a television and modern air conditioner. As an added bonus, there is a small cafe on the ground floor of the building, serving wonderful sandwiches during the day. Some English is spoken. Landlord asks 30 CUC per night.

5) Casa Enrique Montel: Calle 27 #506, altos, entre E y F. Tel (537)832 1807 Cell 53(5)805 0410
A completely independent, 1 bedroom, second floor apartment with an immense, private balcony. The apartment has a large, open living room, an equally large dining room, and a bedroom at the back with a modern en-suite bathroom. The apartment also has a well equipped kitchen. A television and shared phone is provided. The total area of the apartment is about 700 sq.ft, and the balcony is 150 sq.ft. Guests are given the keys and can come and go as they wish. The landlord, Enrique, lives in an adjacent apartment and gives his guests complete privacy. Some English is spoken. Landlord asks 40 CUC per night.

6) <u>Casa Boris And Nora:</u> Calle A #555, entre 23 y 25. Tel (537)833 8806

A completely private apartment located on the second floor of a renovated mansion. The apartment has a massive private terrace, spanning over 1000 sq.ft, overlooking the Vedado neighborhood. The apartment itself consists of a large bedroom with a large, en-suite bathroom, as well as a living room (total size 400 sq.ft.) There is also a kitchen, located beside the apartment, which opens out onto the terrace. Despite being a completely independent apartment, the landlord, Nora, prefers not to give out the keys to the main front gate of the house. She will open the door for you each time you enter the mansion, even if it is late at night. She has no problem doing it. There is a shared phone line in the unit. If needed, there is also another private bedroom (150 sq.ft) located on the second floor which can be rented in conjunction with the main apartment. Also note that there is a small cafe operating throughout the day at the house's main entrance, so cheap food is always available and during the day you can use the cafe area to walk in and out of the property without having to ring the doorbell. Some English is spoken. Landlord asks 30 CUC per night, per room.

7) <u>Casa Mara:</u> Calle 29 #210, entre B y C. Tel (537)830 0382, Cell 53(5)264 6621

A completely independent, second floor apartment, in the heart of Vedado. You have your own front door, with your own set of keys. A spiral staircase leads you to a large and elegantly decorated, one bedroom apartment, located within easy walking distance to all the Vedado attractions. The apartment is new and extremely clean. It spans a total of approximately 300 sq.ft. These is a lot of competition to rent this apartment, so guests should make reservations well in advance of their trip. Some English and French is spoken. Landlord asks 35 CUC per night.

8) <u>Casa Ivelis:</u> Calle 21 #260, Apt 3, entre J y I. Tel (537)832 0071, Cell 53(5)332 5237

A massive, third floor (penthouse) apartment overlooking the whole Vedado neighborhood, with a large front balcony facing south and windows in every room of the house. The apartment has over 1000 sq.ft of living area. It is completely independent and private. The landlord lives on the other side of town and has almost no interaction with the guests. There are two bedrooms to rent in this apartment. If you are renting only one bedroom, Ivelis will not rent out the other room to a different guest. This ensures that you always have complete privacy, regardless if you take both rooms or only one. If you rent just one room, you will have complete use of the whole apartment for the duration of your stay. The apartment has a well equipped kitchen, a large bathroom and a smaller powder room. The living room is equipped with a private phone, television, modern sofas, and a piano. Privacy, luxury and elegance, this apartment has it all. Landlord asks 40 CUC per room, or 60 CUC for both rooms, per night.

9) Casa Maximo: Calle C #660, Apt 2, entre 27 y 29. Tel (537)830 0132, Cell 53(5)264 1651
Two large, completely independent, ground floor apartments. The first apartment has a massive, enclosed, private living area with tons of natural light and several modern rocking chairs and benches. At the back, there is a large bedroom, a good sized bathroom and a kitchen area. The second apartment is located within the main house and includes a large private lounge space (150 sq.ft) plus a completely independent bedroom with en-suite bathroom. You can rent the rooms separately or rent both units together. The major selling point for this casa is the huge, semi-enclosed, atrium living space which gives you all the privacy and independence of a living room, while still providing the sunlight and fresh air of an outdoor terrace. The landlord, Maximo, also has a modern car and offers city tours, taxi services, and economical transportation to the countryside or other Cuban provinces. Some English is spoken. Landlord asks 35 CUC per night, per room.

10) Casa Alexander y Margarita - Private Apartment: Calle 25 #806, entre B y C. Cell 53(5)268 5506
A completely private and independent, two storey apartment, located in a majestic and breathtaking mansion. This apartment used to be

the coach house where the chauffeur of the mansion lived. It has been completely renovated and modernized. On the first floor there is a large living area with a fridge, sofas and dining table. Upstairs there is a modern bedroom with en-suite bathroom. The entire apartment is about 350 sq.ft and is completely independent from the main mansion. The guests get their own keys and can come and go in total privacy. There is also a large driveway which the guests can use as an outdoor space or to park a vehicle. The landlord, Alexander, also has access to a vehicle and can offer city tours, taxi services and economical transportation to the countryside or other Cuban provinces. Some English is spoken. Landlord asks 40 CUC per night.

11) <u>Casa Tania Mendez Calas</u>: Calle 21 #253, Apt 3, entre J y I. Tel (537)832 9283, Cell 53(5)345 5179

A large, 1 bedroom apartment, located on the second floor of a modern building. Very close to the action, yet still located on a very quiet street. The bedroom has 2 queen beds, so it is a great option for couples traveling with children. The apartment has a full living room, kitchen and large, glass-enclosed balcony. The bedroom has an en-suite bathroom. In total, the living area is about 500 sq.ft. The apartment is completely independent. Guests have all the keys and can come and go as they wish. The landlord, Tania, lives just down the street and is always available to answer questions or give advice. Some English is spoken. Landlord asks 35 CUC per night.

12) <u>Casa Julio Cesar</u>: Calle I #513, esquina 25. Tel (537)832 0786, Cell 53(5)284 0607

Totally independent apartment on the third floor of a huge mansion. The apartment has 2 bedrooms which can be rented together or separately. Total apartment size is about 800 sq.ft. It includes a long terrace, a large open concept living room and dining room and a well equipped, modern kitchen. Rooms are large and have air conditioning, televisions and a fridge. Located on a quiet street with little traffic or noise, but only one block to La Rampa. A very modern looking apartment for a fantastic price. Some English and French is spoken. Landlord asks only 35 CUC per night.

13) Casa Estela Navarro: Paseo #651, esquina 27 (entrance and doorbell on 27th). Tel (537)836 6656, Cell 53(5)325 7210
This apartment is located on the second floor of a restored colonial mansion. It has its own entrance and is completely independent from the main house. The guests receive the keys and they can come and go in complete privacy. The apartment is about 350 sq.ft and includes a large bedroom with a television and fridge. There is a living room/dining room and a small kitchen. The apartment has its own phone line. The best part about this casa is the massive terrace overlooking Ave. Paseo, with a view of the Plaza de la Revolución. The terrace measures over 1000 sq.ft. There is also an outdoor laundry area beside the terrace. This casa really has it all. The landlord speaks some English, French, Italian and Russian. Landlord asks 40 CUC per night, but the price is negotiable for stays over 1 week.

14) Casa Myrna: Calle 27 # 755, entre Paseo y A. Tel (537)831 7425, Cell 53(5)274 8883
An apartment of about 400 sq.ft, with one large closed bedroom, as well as a living area, bathroom and kitchen. In the front, there is a private terrace and a gated yard area. For all practical purposes, this unit is completely independent and guests are provided the keys so that they can enter and exit at will. The landlord, Myrna, lives in a completely separate part of the house, located at the rear of the building. Due to the layout of the unit, the guests share a common front door with the landlord. This apartment is new on the rental market and offers a degree of elegance and charm which is rare in Havana. The location is central while still being very private and quiet. Landlord asks only 30 CUC per night.

Closing Notes: If you ever find yourself in Havana without a casa reservation, I suggest calling any of the casas particulares on this list. The landlords will always help you to find accommodations, even if they themselves do not have a vacancy.

As mentioned before, to view photos of all the casas particulares presented in this guide and to quickly and easily <u>book all your reservations online</u>, simply check out the website

www.BestCubaGuide.com

Also, on this website, make sure to check out the <u>forum</u>, where you will find lots more information, money saving tips and deals, and answers to all your Cuba and Havana travel questions.

Notes:

_____
_____
_____
_____
_____
_____
_____
_____
_____
_____
_____
_____
_____
_____
_____
_____
_____
_____
_____

Have a wonderful trip!